THE NEW MOLE

THE NEW MOLE

PATHS OF THE LATIN AMERICAN LEFT

———◆———

EMIR SADER

Translated by
Iain Bruce

VERSO
London • New York

Consejo Latinoamericano
de Ciencias Sociales **CLACSO** Conselho Latino-americano
de Ciências Sociais

Editor in Chief: Emir Sader – Executive Secretary of CLACSO

Academic Coordinator: Pablo Gentili – Assistant Executive Secretary of CLACSO

Production and Web Content Department

Editor: Lucas Sablich
Art Director: Marcelo Giardino

Latin American Social Sciences Council – Consejo Latinoamericano de Ciencias Sociales – Conselho Latino-americano de Ciências Sociais
Av. Callao 875 | piso 4° G| C1023AAB Ciudad de Buenos Aires | Argentina
Tel (54 11) 4811 6588 | Fax (54 11) 4812 8459 | clacso@clacso.edu.ar |
www.clacso.org

CLACSO receives support from the Swedish International Development Cooperation Agency (SIDA) Asdi

First published by Verso 2011
© Verso 2011
Translation © Iain Bruce 2011
First published as *A Nova Toupeira:*
Os Caminhos da Esquerda Latino-Americana
© Ed. Boitempo 2009

1 3 5 7 9 10 8 6 4 2

Verso
UK: 6 Meard Street, London W1F 0EG
US: 20 Jay Street, Suite 1010, Brooklyn, NY 11201
www.versobooks.com

Verso is the imprint of New Left Books

ISBN-13: 978-1-84467-692-7

British Library Cataloguing in Publication Data
A catalogue record for this book is available from the British Library

Library of Congress Cataloging-in-Publication Data
A catalog record for this book is available from the Library of Congress

Typeset by MJ Gavan, Cornwall
Printed in the US by Maple Vail

Contents

THE PATHS

The paths,
the paths did not make themselves
when man,
when man stopped dragging himself.

The paths,
the paths finally met
when man,
when man was no longer alone.

The paths,
the paths that we find made
are leftovers,
are leftovers of former neighbours.

Let us not take not take
those paths
because they are only,
they are only dead paths.

Pablo Milanés

It is necessary to dream, but only on the condition that we seriously believe in our dream, that we examine real life with care, that we compare our observations with our dream and that we realize our phantasy scrupulously.

Vladimir Lenin

Introduction: Half a Century

What is happening in Latin America? In the first decade of the twenty-first century, a series of governments and movements have emerged across the region, establishing themselves as an alternative to the neoliberal consensus that prevailed in the 1990s. Why did this new left appear in Latin America, what are its characteristics, and what forms has its struggle taken?

We decided to call this book *The New Mole*, in reference to a passage in Karl Marx's *Eighteenth Brumaire of Louis Bonaparte*. After describing how the class confrontation in France seemed to have ended in a stalemate of mutual defeat, with all classes prostrate before the 'rifle butt', he continued:

> But the revolution is thoroughgoing. It is still travelling through purgatory. It does its work methodically ... And when it has accomplished this second half of its preliminary work, Europe will leap from its seat and exult: Well burrowed, old mole![1]

---

1. Karl Marx, *The Eighteenth Brumaire of Louis Bonaparte*, collected in *Surveys From Exile*, London 2010 [1852], p. 237. In this final chapter Marx paraphrases Shakespeare's *Hamlet*, Act 1, Scene 5: 'Well said, old mole, canst work i' th' earth so fast? A worthy pioneer!'

Marx conjured the image of that small, almost blind animal which moves around below ground unbeknownst to us, and then suddenly appears where we least we expect it. The mole burrows away silently, ceaselessly, even while order reigns on the surface and there is nothing to suggest approaching turbulence. It is an image that captures the permanent contradictions inherent in capitalism, contradictions that continue to operate even when 'social peace' – that of the bayonets, of the cemetery and of alienation – seems to prevail. Hegel spoke of the tricks and surprises of history in similar vein: 'Great revolutions which strike the eye at a glance must have been preceded by a still and secret revolution in the spirit of the age, a revolution not visible to every eye.'[2]

Marx has been called the 'great detector of signs'. To grasp how reality moves is to decipher the course of its contradictions. Lenin did this when he identified Russia as the 'weakest link in the imperialist chain' at the beginning of the twentieth century. There, the contradictions of the imperialist system could be found in concentrated form. Lenin saw how the structures of power could be fractured in backward Russia, without abandoning Marx's central idea that socialism would be built by overcoming – and negating – the contradictions generated by unequal and combined development. He observed that it was easier to take power on the periphery, but much more difficult to build socialism – hence the expectation that advanced Germany would come to the rescue of backward Russia.

After 1917, the weakest link seemed to be Germany, defeated in the war, its reconstruction blocked by draconian armistice agreements. The failure of the German Revolution (1918–1923) strongly influenced not only the process of building socialism in the Soviet Union, but all the early expressions of socialism in the twentieth century. The Soviet Union was isolated, and the old mole – which had surfaced so suddenly in Russia – moved even further from the centre of capitalism. Instead of breaking out in developed Western Europe, it found

---

2. G. W. F. Hegel, *Early Theological Writings*, Philadelphia 1971, p. 152.

more fertile soil in backward Asia, in China, then in Vietnam, and later emerged in a commodity-exporting country – Cuba – in another peripheral continent. As always, it appeared where it was less difficult to break the chain of imperial domination – not least because of the surprise factor – but where it was also more difficult to build socialism, because the productive forces were less developed.

The mole's comings and goings were becoming increasingly unpredictable, with revolutions breaking out in the most unexpected places and forms. Writing of the May 1968 outburst in Paris, Sartre referred to the 'fear of revolution' felt by communists, who were always looking for new assaults on the Winter Palace as the sign that a revolution was breaking out. Sartre merely repeated Gramsci's description of the Russian Revolution as 'a revolution against *Capital*', not to belittle it or to diminish its anti-capitalist character, but in order to point out how all new revolutionary processes appear in heterodox fashion and seem to contradict rather than confirm the predictions of socialist theorists – only to end up rewriting the same script in a different way.

Two centuries after the wars of independence, one century after the Mexican Revolution, half a century after the Cuban Revolution, the new mole has re-emerged spectacularly in the continent of José Martí, Bolívar, Sandino, Farabundo Martí, Mariátegui, Fidel, Che and Allende; it has taken on new forms in order to continue the centuries-old struggle for emancipation of the peoples of Latin America and the Caribbean. Understanding this new path and the novel forms and rhythms adopted is a necessary condition for being in step with our time. If history now moves forward in disguise, the task for theory is to decipher these new manifestations of the contradictions that characterize the systems of exploitation, domination and alienation, so that we can see how to build up the economic, social, political and ideological strength needed for a renewal of revolutionary processes in today's world.

*   *   *

The original publication of this book coincided with the fiftieth anniversary of the Cuban Revolution, as well as marking fifty years since the start of my own political activism. In my case, the two are closely interlinked. In 1959, when I was in the first year of pre-university at the Brasílio Machado State College in Vila Mariana, a middle-class neighbourhood of São Paulo, I read Marxist authors and took part in the secondary-school student movement; later I was president of the São Paulo Secondary-School Students' Union (UPES). It was at that time that my older brother Eder and I met Michael Löwy, who was teaching at a public university in the interior of São Paulo state. He invited us to a meeting of a socialist group, the Independent Socialist League (LSI), which saw itself as Marxist, Leninist and Luxemburgist; its leader, Hermínio Sachetta, had been expelled from the Communist Party. The League had a minuscule headquarters in the old quarter of São Paulo, down an alleyway that was known as the last stop on one of the tram lines – the Asdrúbal do Nascimento. In this space of not more than ten square metres there was room for just one bench on either side and a table at the end by the window, where Sachetta would sit. I remember him with a stubby red pencil, scribbling on a piece of paper as he talked. The first task we were given, as the three new members of the LSI, was to distribute the organization's paper. It was called *Socialist Action*. There on the front page was the photo of bearded guerrillas, posing as if they were in a football team, celebrating the fall of a dictator in a place that we knew, generically, as 'Central America'.

The Cuban Revolution, and the historical process that followed it, have left such a deep mark on this last half century that it is no longer possible to understand a large part of the lives of several generations without them. The 'Cold War' only served to increase this impact when it turned Cuba, along with a divided Berlin, into one of two points of contact between the two systems – the capitalist and the socialist – of a polarized world. Until then, for us in Brazil and Latin America, socialism had been something very distant, that happened in Asia and was inhabited by legendary, almost supernatural figures like Lenin and Mao Zedong. We thought we knew about some revolutions – genuine or not – like the Mexican Revolution and the Revolution of 1930 in Brazil, but we barely mentioned the Bolivian Revolution of 1952. The meaning of the word remained imprecise and unclear; it was the French Revolution that provided the classic point of reference, even though its relevance was limited to the transition from feudalism to capitalism.

While the programmes of the left tried to give concrete, national roots to both socialism and communism, both remained mere conjectures, things we could only read about. We read *The Communist Manifesto* and *Socialism: Utopian and Scientific*. We knew of the heroic, defeated experience of the Paris Commune, because we'd read *The Civil War in France*. We'd read *Ten Days that Shook the World*, and some also got stuck into Trotsky's *History of the Russian Revolution*, or even Isaac Deutscher's prophet trilogy.[3] Our ideas of the struggle for socialism were guided more by an image of insurrection associated with the October Revolution and the storming of the Winter Palace, than by the experiences of guerrilla movements in China or Vietnam – which only began to exist for us in the 1960s. We were unaware of Dien Bien Phu and the Yugoslav, Albanian or Korean guerrillas.

It took only a small country – a Caribbean island, dependent on the single commodity export of sugar, and just ninety miles from the USA – to put socialism on the agenda for Latin America and the Western hemisphere, and in the process to radically change the direction of contemporary history and the lives of millions of people.

The Cuban Revolution and the political activism of the new generations were the product of a new period in world history. If the counter-revolution had been in the ascendant during the first half of the century, the political climate changed after the Second World War, with the defeat of fascism, the creation of

---

3. Isaac Deutscher published the three-volume biography of Trotsky as *The Prophet Armed* in 1952, *The Prophet Unarmed* in 1959 and *The Prophet Outcast* in 1963.

the socialist camp in Eastern Europe, the start of movements for independence in Africa and Asia, starting with India, and above all the victory of the Chinese Revolution. Fidel Castro and Che Guevara were the figures who seemed to embody this changed climate. You could almost say that the generations that followed would be defined by their position in relation to these two.

In *Les rendez-vous manqués* (Missed Encounters), Régis Debray questions the destiny of a part of his own generation which was looking for revolution – a revolution that Europe denied them and which they went to search for in Latin America. As part of this encounter with revolution, Debray recounts the adventures of Pierre Goldman, a less fortunate comrade who tried to join up with the guerrillas in Venezuela and ended up being murdered in Paris by a far-right death squad; in a letter written earlier, Goldman had anticipated that one day, 'we will be grateful that we were twenty in the 1960s'.

The events of the 1960s convinced us that the left was destined for victory. Being on the left meant being anti-capitalist, socialist, Marxist, Guevarist. 'Either socialist revolution or a caricature of revolution', that was the slogan we lived by. Marxism, which we adopted very early on, provided the backbone of our studies: 'the philosophers have only interpreted the world, in various ways, the point is to change it',[4] not least because 'theory also becomes a material force as soon as it has gripped the masses'.[5] For us, there seemed to be a mutual reinforcement between being Marxist and the movement of history that put revolution on the immediate agenda, as if reality and theory were converging in Hegelian fashion. Everything happened because we became Marxists, but everything that happened also pushed us into becoming Marxists.

Today, after so many blows and achievements, so many victories and defeats, setbacks and advances, revolutions

---

4. Thesis XI of Karl Marx, *Theses on Feuerbach*, 1845, in Marx/Engels *Selected Works*, vol. 1, Moscow 1969, pp. 13–15.
5. Karl Marx, 'Introduction' to *A Contribution to the Critique of Hegel's Philosophy of Right*, 1843.

and counter-revolutions, what sense is there still for political activism, socialism, the left, revolution? What do Che, Marx, Gramsci, Lenin, revolutionary theory, Marxism, all mean now? Up until the collapse of the communist world, we knew that we were not condemned to capitalism, that since 1917, a part of humanity had chosen socialism. Yet in the end, capitalism did not give way to socialism; the first attempts at the latter reverted to savage varieties of the former. History was much more open than we had imagined; the challenges were much greater than we had anticipated.

To some extent, the principle that 'the wheel of history does not go backwards' was accepted by all those who adopted Marxism in one or other of its variants. All of us were marked by the assumption that 'the higher stage of capitalism', represented by imperialism, was its final phase, destined to disappear in a relatively short space of time. The big debate in the 1970s – that's just thirty years ago – was not whether capitalism was condemned to disappear, but how and when this would happen. Even those who never accepted determinism or economism – the assumption that history was marching inexorably from one mode of production to another, each superior to the last, from primitive communism, through slavery, feudalism and capitalism, and eventually arriving at socialism – never imagined the possibility that the Soviet Union and the socialist camp might simply disappear and return to capitalism.

For the left, this falling out of step with history has been the biggest ideological and psychological shock to the system. People sought refuge in many places: in a return to the original, pure Marx; in replacing socialism with democracy as the ultimate political objective; in abandoning any aspiration to collectively changing the world; in a retreat into the private sphere, almost always with the excuse that the dreams of socialism have failed. It is as if the left were transported from the future into the past, from anticipating what was to come to witnessing what has already been. It is as if capitalism – in its US version – had snatched the future out of our hands and thrown us into the world of technology, advertising and consumption, imprisoning us in the past – 'the passing of an illusion', according to a new, born-again anti-communism.

At the height of its triumph, capitalism has shown itself to be more unjust than ever. The more deregulated it gets, the crueller it gets, taking away elementary rights like the right to formal employment. Capital today turns everything into a commodity, whether education or health care or water. Just as it concentrates income and property even more, just as it subordinates production to speculation, marginalizes and excludes the majority of the world's population, fosters war and ecological destruction, at the same time capital puts on its most complacent expression. For with the disappearance of socialism from the contemporary historical agenda, capital meets little resistance; its rule goes almost unchallenged. Nonetheless, it is capitalism itself that puts all the themes of anti-capitalist struggle – and therefore of socialism – back on the agenda. It seems that as long as capitalism exists, socialism too must hover on the horizon as an alternative, potential or real; because, in the last analysis, it is just this, anti-capitalism, its dialectical negation.

In the light of all this, can we expect the mole to return? Does it have anything more to say to us? This book seeks to give voice to the mole. At the beginning of this twenty-first century, only it can recover the thread of history from the particular forms of present-day anti-capitalist struggle. Revolution never repeats itself; it always appears as a heretic. To follow the steps of the mole, to take up once again the task of 'sniffing out the signs', as Marx did, is to rediscover the threads that connect, in contradictory ways, the reality of today with our future.

The mole moves between earth and the heavens, between darkness and light, between the depths and the surface. When it retires into the bowels of the earth, it is not to hibernate but to keep on digging, deeper and deeper. It never returns by the way it came, but always opens up a new and different path. When it cannot be seen, it is not because it has disappeared; it has simply become invisible. The mole is forever digging.

The New Mole

Once again in Latin America, a century gets off to a surprising start. The beginning of the nineteenth was marked by an impressive cycle of independence revolutions – from 1810 to 1822 – from which only Brazil, Cuba and Puerto Rico were exempt. Interestingly, the latter two would have the most diametrically opposed destinies on the continent: the first, socialist, the second, as virtually an extra star on the United States' flag. These independence wars produced a generation of great popular leaders – from Bolívar to Sucre, from San Martín to O'Higgins, from Toussaint Louverture to Francia – who led the process of expelling the colonialists, founding national states and eliminating slavery.

In spite of the importance of these changes for our continent and for each of our countries, Latin America did not acquire a prominent role in world history. We continued to fulfil a number of functions that were vital for the development of European capitalism, as suppliers of agricultural products and raw materials, as consumer markets and as a source of cheap labour, without, however, playing a high-profile part on the international political stage.

The following century burst onto the scene in explosive fashion, with the massacre of miners at the Santa María School in Iquique, northern Chile (1907), the Mexican Revolution (1910) and the Córdoba university reform movement (1918), thus putting firmly on our political agenda proletarian, agrarian and educational questions. A new generation of popular leaders emerged in the history of the region: Zapata, Pancho Villa, Luis Emilio Recabarren, Sandino, Farabundo Martí, Julio Antonio Mella, José Carlos Mariátegui and Luis Carlos Prestes, among others. A century of revolutions and counter-revolutions was on the way for Latin America.

This situation lasted right through the twentieth century, with such explosive potential translating into major political experiences. The continent ceased to be a collection of primary commodity exporters ruled by traditional political oligarchies. Various national states grew stronger, by concentrating more on their domestic markets and through a deepening social and nationalist awareness. It was to be a century marked by nationalist governments, military coups, socialist projects – for the first time in the history of the region – and by neoliberal governments.

The continent where neoliberalism was first applied – in Chile and Bolivia – had the further privilege of becoming, quite soon, the site of greatest resistance to that same neoliberalism, and of the most developed alternatives to it. These are, of course, two sides of the same coin. As the laboratory of neoliberal experiments, Latin America was one of the first to feel their consequences, and therefore became the weakest link in the neoliberal chain.

The 1990s and the 2000s were two radically opposite decades. During the '90s, the neoliberal model was imposed to varying degrees in virtually every country on the continent – with the exception of Cuba – in apparent confirmation of the Washington Consensus and its slogan, 'There Is No Alternative'. Military dictatorships in some of the most politically influential countries, like those of the Southern Cone, had prepared the way for this imposition of neoliberal hegemony in every part of the region.

Bill Clinton, who did not even cross the Río Grande to sign the first North American Free Trade Agreement (NAFTA), was forced not long after to approve a super-loan from Washington when the first crisis of the new model broke out in Mexico. No other country in Latin America got a visit from Clinton during his first term; the region was doing just as it was told, by Washington, by the World Bank, by the International Monetary Fund (IMF) and by the World Trade Organization (WTO). The US went on to press for a hemisphere-wide Free Trade Area of the Americas (FTAA), presenting this as the natural outcome of the seamless extension of free-trade policies.

At an Americas summit meeting in Quebec in April 2001, Venezuela's Hugo Chávez was the only leader to vote against Clinton's proposal for an FTAA, while Cardoso, Menem, Fujimori and their colleagues fell meekly into line. Soon after this, on the occasion of his first Ibero-American Summit, Chávez reported, Castro passed him a piece of paper on which he had written: 'At last I'm not the only devil around here.' It was thus with some relief, too, that Chávez – himself elected president of Venezuela in 1998 – attended the investiture of Lula in Brasilia and Néstor Kirchner in Buenos Aires in 2003, before moving on to that of Tabaré Vázquez in Montevideo in 2004, that of Evo Morales in La Paz in 2006, and in 2007 those of Daniel Ortega in Managua and Rafael Correa in Quito; followed in 2008 by Fernando Lugo in Asunción. Meanwhile the US free trade proposal that had been almost unanimously approved in 2000 was dead and buried by the end of 2005. Since then, both Chávez and Lula had been re-elected, in 2006, while Kirchner had been succeeded by his wife in 2008.

What can explain such a radical shift, of a kind the continent had never experienced in all its history, with so many governments that can be described as progressive (of the left or centre-left, according to criteria that we shall discuss further on)? What does Latin America and the Caribbean look like after all these changes? How far does neoliberalism remain hegemonic, or can we say that it has entered what might be called a 'post-neoliberal' period? In which case, what characterizes these new Latin American governments? What are the strengths that the anti-neoliberal struggle can draw on, and what are the obstacles it faces? What projections can we make about the future of the continent in the first half of the twenty-first century?

The American continent has the biggest inequalities in the world, and therefore the biggest injustices – a situation that only got worse in the neoliberal decade. Yet the heavy blows suffered by the popular forces, both at the hands of dictatorships and directly from neoliberal policies, made rapid and deep change seem unlikely. We will seek to understand the conditions that enabled such a radical change and turned a neoliberal paradise into an anti-neoliberal oasis (in a wider world still dominated by the neoliberal model), but also the potential and limits of this change in a regional and international context.

CYCLES OF THE LATIN AMERICAN MOLE

Latin American history is full of surprises, for anyone who cannot understand its peculiar, underlying movement. The wars of independence are too often seen as extensions of the Independence Revolution in the United States. But this fails to grasp their popular dimension, the way they united the forces for independence around an anti-colonial identity – with the contributions of Bolívar, Martí, Artigas, Toussaint Louverture, among many others – focused on abolishing slavery, introducing Republics and beginning to build nation-states.

Popular rebellions like those led by Tupac Amaru and Tupac Katari in Peru, the Haitian Revolution led by Toussaint Louverture, guerrilla movements like that of Manuel Rodríguez or the Carrera brothers in Chile, along with other popular movements involving aboriginal peoples and blacks, had already shown the strength of the masses that ran through the region's history. Whilst in the United States, slavery survived and coexisted with independence – when they invaded and annexed Mexican territories, the USA reintroduced slavery into Texas – the end of the colonial period in Latin America automatically meant its abolition. Brazil, which went from being a colony to being a monarchy, instead of a republic, and Cuba, which did not achieve independence until the beginning of the twentieth century, were exceptions.

Among its sharpest, most aware representatives, like Simón Bolívar and José Martí, this powerful, national movement for independence already pointed towards a confrontation with the United States. Bolívar had already criticized this anachronism in the post-independence US, when he stated, in 1820: 'It seems to me like madness that a revolution carried out in the name of freedom should seek to preserve slavery.'[1] With extraordinary foresight, he added: 'The United States seems destined by providence to drown our America in misfortune.'[2]

A few decades later, in 1895, Martí, basing himself on his own experience of life and politics in the United States, wrote these lines:

> I am in daily danger of giving my life for my country and duty … the duty of preventing in time, through Cuban independence, the United States from spreading through the Antilles and from overpowering with that additional strength our lands of America. All I have done so far, and all I will do, is for this purpose … to prevent the opening in Cuba (through annexation by the imperialists from there and the Spaniards) of the road that must be closed, and that we are closing with our blood, that which leads to to the annexation of our American nations to the brutal and turbulent North which despises them … I have lived in the monster and I know its entrails; my sling is David's.[3]

Bolívar and Martí's early awareness of the era of imperialist domination that was just beginning, anticipated how the country that had been unable to win independence from Spain

---

1. Manoel Lelo Belotto and Anna Maria Martinez Corrêa (eds), *Bolívar*, São Paulo 1983, p. 20.
2. Ibid.
3. From José Martí's last, unfinished letter to Manuel Mercado, 18 May 1895, also known as his Testament. The following day, Martí was killed fighting the Spanish at Dos Ríos.

at the beginning of the nineteenth century, would have to confront emerging imperialism at the end of the century to obtain its independence. This fusion of national and social questions would help Cuba – an island located 140 kilometres from the greatest imperial power in the history of humanity – to break the imperial chain at one of its most unexpected links.

Cuba was a commodity-exporting country, with an economy based on sugar and almost entirely dependent on the US market. Yet the Revolution was to give it an unprecedented international role throughout the second half of the twentieth century. A new 'revolution against *Capital*', a new and sudden appearance of the old mole, confirmed that revolutions are only possible when they break the established strategic rules – rules that are assumed to be obligatory, until the concrete logic of concrete reality pushes them aside.

It was the strength of national feeling that led Cuba to join the wave of struggles which swept the continent at the beginning of the nineteenth century, with the weakening of Spanish rule as a result of the Napoleonic invasions and the influence of the US War of Independence. However this feeling did not triumph, because the radical character of the movement made the elites fearful of losing control over it. After a first attempt at launching an independence war in the 1870s, Cuba gathered sufficient forces to defeat Spanish colonialism. But this second attempt, already under the leadership of Martí, was aborted in 1895 by the intervention of the emerging imperial power of the United States. Cuba had to pay the price for failing to throw off Spanish domination decades earlier, and now confronted the United States in its new imperialist role. The island saw the creation of what historians have called a 'proto-republic', supervised by the US.

The impossibility of solving the national question meant that this banner was later added, by the 1959 revolution, to those of anti-imperialist, anti-capitalist and socialist change. That is why nationalism and socialism are so profoundly entwined in the Cuban movement. It is a result of the weight of US domination in Cuba's history.

The victory of the Cuban Revolution was the biggest surprise ever experienced in Latin America's history. In the second half of the 1950s the classic movements of nationalism were in full retreat, with the fall of Getúlio Vargas and Juan Perón, as well as the degeneration of the Bolivian and Mexican revolutions. The latter had begun earlier, in parallel with the return of large-scale US investments following a long interregnum provoked by the crisis of 1929, the Second World War and the Korean War. Throughout the continent, left-wing parties seemed bereft of prospects, either because they had been isolated by the Cold War, or because they were dependent on declining nationalist movements.

The attack on the Moncada barracks in 1953, and later the landing of the boat, the Granma, in 1957, were seen as 'adventurist deviations', events that did not fit the pre-established path of history, which had not just a script, but an already identified cast and directors. People had forgotten about the unpredictable mole, who therefore had surprise on its side.

Equally or even more surprising was the course followed by the victorious revolution, which moved rapidly from the democratic phase to the anti-imperialist and anti-capitalist phase, sped on by the dynamic between revolution and counter-revolution that affects all genuinely revolutionary processes. This was the unequal battle from which Cuba emerged victorious. Until then in Latin America, all governments that came into conflict with US interests had been defeated, either by military coups or through capitulation. No country had successfully confronted the United States, not even the relatively more powerful ones like Mexico, Argentina and Brazil. No one could have expected this small country to come out the winner.

There came into play what Trotsky called the 'privilege of backwardness', plus what Lenin referred to as 'the weakest link in the chain', both of them manifestations of the law of uneven and combined development. Since Mexico, Brazil and Argentina were seen by the United States as the countries most liable to escape its sphere of influence and upset the balance of forces in the region, that is where Washington concentrated its efforts to contain what it saw as communist activity in the region. The traditional cold-war mechanisms which had isolated Cuba's communist party, the Popular Socialist Party (PSP), seemed to have the situation under control. No anti-dictatorial movement in the region, not even those opposing US allies, had escaped such control.

The absence of surprise helped to prevent other victories in Latin America in the decades that followed, even with the spread of guerrilla movements from Mexico to Uruguay, from Guatemala to Argentina or Brazil. All forms of dissent were dealt with – in this framework of the Cold War and National Security Doctrine – as 'subversive', as 'infiltrated' from abroad, as an external virus that had penetrated the body of society and needed to be stamped out.

Such action was backed up by the so-called Alliance for Progress, put forward by the United States to encourage reforms in the countryside and to promote smallholder and medium-sized farming, as a way of reducing contradictions and containing peasant mobilizations. Something similar had been imposed in Japan and South Korea, under US military occupation, in order to prevent the spread of agrarian revolutions like that which had occurred in China.

Chile was, during the Christian Democrat government of Eduardo Frei, the country chosen by the Alliance for Progress to showcase what it called its 'revolution in freedom', to distinguish it from the Cuban revolution. But Frei's agrarian reform did not prosper, his government was a failure and the mole was able to resurface with the socialist government of Salvador Allende.

Now that guerrilla movements were blocked, the mole responded by promoting institutional governments – that of Velasco Alvarado in Peru in 1969, that of Allende in 1970. Two of the most important bastions of conservative power in the region began to be penetrated by progressive ideas: Peru's armed forces, a foretaste of what would happen in Venezuela three decades later, and the Catholic Church, with the Second

Vatican Council and Liberation Theology, which spread through most countries in the continent.

In Chile, the question of power and the contradiction between democracy and capitalism would be posed explicitly. In the country with the longest tradition of institutional stability in the region, an alliance of communists and socialists (Popular Unity) won the presidential election in 1970, after the failure of the governments of a conservative, Jorge Alessandri (1958–1964), and Eduardo Frei (1964–1970). This alliance, after four previous attempts, now won with just 36.3 per cent of the vote.

Until then in Latin America, progressive governments *had* been elected, particularly those of a nationalist character, such as the governments of Vargas in Brazil in 1950, Perón in Argentina in 1945 and 1950, and Lázaro Cárdenas in Mexico in 1936. Chile itself had elected, in 1938, one of the world's three Popular Front governments (the other two were in France and Spain) presided by Pedro Aguirre Cerda, in which the young doctor Salvador Allende served as Minister of Health. But Allende was the first to win with a socialist programme promising anti-capitalist changes (there had been, at the beginning of the 1930s, another Chilean government that proclaimed itself socialist, which survived in office for just twelve days[4]).

It was not by chance that these experiments unfolded in Chile, which was a kind of Latin American 'political laboratory', to use the phrase that Engels applied to France. The roots of these peculiarities go back a long way, and have to do with the institutional tradition of the political system and the relatively early emergence of the workers' movement in Chile.

Once the country had been united, back in 1830, under the iron hand of Portales – while other countries in the region remained embroiled in major internal conflicts – Chile proceeded to elect all its presidents until the military coup of 1973, with the exceptions of 1891 and the period from 1924 to 1931. The country established a Congress before any

---

4. The so-called Socialist Republic of Chile lasted from 4 to 16 June, 1932.

country in Europe, except Britain and Norway. In the middle of the nineteenth century, electoral participation in Chile was equivalent to that in Holland at the time, a level that Britain had achieved only twenty years earlier, and which Italy would achieve only twenty years later. Chile introduced secret ballots in 1874, before Belgium, Denmark, Norway and France.

At the same time the country had a relatively developed workers' movement, compared with other countries in the region. Although all of them were commodity-exporting economies, Chile exported minerals – tin and later copper. Instead of an extended peasantry, it developed a concentrated working class of miners. Already, by the end of the nineteenth century, there was a proletariat that gave birth to a strong workers' movement, even before there was a real industrial bourgeoisie.

In 1920, Luis Emilio Recabarren, founder of the Chilean and Argentinean Communist Parties, stood for President. In 1938 there was the Popular Front government. The Eduardo Frei administration was the Alliance for Progress's pilot project for Latin America, and that of Allende was the world's first experience of an institutional transition to socialism. The 1973 coup brought to power the most significant military dictatorship of the period, for it was there that neoliberalism began to be introduced in Latin America and the world.

The oil crisis, the same year as the coups in Chile and Uruguay, marked the end of the long wave of postwar capitalist expansion, through which the United States had consolidated its leading position in the Western bloc; now it would use the transition to a new model to revitalize that role.

The mole's next appearance – with the Sandinista victory in Nicaragua – came in the context of a long, recessive cycle and the beginnings of a fresh international offensive by the United States, following its defeat in Vietnam, the Watergate scandal and Richard Nixon's resignation. The brief parenthesis represented by the Carter administration came to a rapid close with fresh US defeats in 1979 – the revolutions in Iran, Nicaragua and Grenada. The Sandinista victory and the guerrilla offensives in El Salvador and Guatemala unfolded against the background of this new balance of international forces, the second Cold War, derived from the Reagan administration's new international offensive.

At first the Sandinistas could count on support and sympathy from governments like those of Mexico (Institutional Revolutionary Party, PRI) or Venezuela (Carlos Andrés Pérez, of Democratic Action), as well as from European social democracy. But this situation was reversed, making it easier for the US to encircle Nicaragua and militarize Honduras, in order to use the latter as a rearguard for the *contras* and for themselves, just as Laos and Cambodia had been used in Indochina to encircle Vietnam.

At first, European social democrats saw Nicaragua as a sort of pluralist counterpoint to what they regarded as the closed model of Cuba. Nonetheless, the international polarization of the second Cold War, with the ferociously anti-Soviet sentiments imposed in Europe by the North Americans, led European social democracy to distance itself from the Sandinista government, and eventually to oppose it.

The climate in the 1980s was not just anti-Soviet, but anti-Cuban, anti-Vietnamese and anti-Nicaraguan – leading Gabriel García Márquez to remark that 'they show solidarity with our defeats, but they cannot stand our victories'. The Pol Pot regime in Cambodia was used as a phantom in the attempt to identify revolution with totalitarianism. The ground was being laid for the new neoliberal hegemony in the arenas of politics and ideology as well.

The North American offensive in Europe left its mark on the left, too. Based on the supposed 'Soviet threat' and an updated theory of totalitarianism – which identified Stalinism with Nazism – social democracy reaffirmed its Atlanticist preference for a subordinated alliance with the United States. The unity of the left was weakened, and Western Europe took an increasing distance from Latin America and the entire capitalist periphery.

One decisive moment in this turn by European social democracy was the change in position adopted by François

Mitterrand, early in his second year in office, when his government abandoned the traditional Keynesianism of the French left and adhered – for the first time in a social-democratic government – to the neoliberal model, strengthening its alliance with the Anglo-Saxon bloc and distancing itself from the south. This coincided, at home, with the breaking of the alliance with the Communist Party. The social-democratic parties of Germany, Holland, France, Spain and Italy exerted a decisive influence on this turn. In Chile, for example, the consequence was direct: the Socialist Party broke its alliance with the communists and signed another – which has lasted to the present day – with the Christian Democrats, forming a bloc that continued the neoliberal economic policies of Pinochet.

In 1989, the same year as the fall of the Berlin Wall, three decisive events showed that the neoliberal model was beginning to be adopted throughout Latin America. These were the electoral victories of Carlos Menem in Argentina, of Fernando Collor de Mello in Brazil and of Carlos Andrés Pérez in Venezuela. The unexpected political and ideological shifts in Peronism and Democratic Action, following that of the PRI in Mexico, showed that nationalist currents, like social democracy, were also adhering to the new model. Neoliberalism was becoming dominant throughout the continent.

In Venezuela, Democratic Action's Pérez was elected for a second time, promising a programme of economic regeneration. Almost immediately he adopted a severe fiscal adjustment package of neoliberal character. There was a massive popular reaction, which became known as the *caracazo* and resulted in hundreds of deaths.

Menem was also elected promising a 'productive revolution', but rapidly appointed Miguel Roig as Economy minister, followed by Néstor Rapanelli – both executives of the Bunge and Born group, and representatives of a business sector traditionally hostile to Peronism. This move, too, indicated the shift to economic liberalism. One of the main pillars of Argentinean identity, Peronism with its nationalist bent, had joined the new Latin American consensus.

In Brazil, Collor de Mello beat Lula in the second round and began the neoliberal cycle, which continued when social democracy, in the person of Fernando Henrique Cardoso, lent its support. In Bolivia, the National Revolutionary Movement – which had headed the 1952 Revolution with Víctor Paz Estenssoro as its historic leader – had begun to apply neoliberalism in 1986 as a response to hyperinflation. In Mexico, too, the model was already up and running: President Carlos Salinas de Gortari – elected in 1988 – took up where his predecessor, Miguel de la Madrid, left off, and the neoliberal banner was later taken over by his successor, Ernesto Zedillo. All three were, of course, members of the PRI, originally a nationalist party.

Successive political and ideological defeats for the left, with all their consequences on the social level, meant prolonged setbacks across the continent. In fact, as progressive parties joined the neoliberal camp, resistance became confined almost exclusively to the social movements. No case was more dramatic than that of Argentina.

Peronism, which had occupied a large part of the political spectrum and of the workers' movement as well, put the neoliberal model into practice in one of the most spectacular ideological U-turns in the region, because it led the bulk of the organized trade union movement to follow the same path. This limited the space for resistance and facilitated the most radical process of privatizations ever seen in Latin America. The backdrop – reflected in people's everyday lives – was a monetary stabilization plan, introduced after two crises of hyperinflation, that entailed parity with the dollar. This artificially raised the purchasing power of the Argentinean currency, creating a time-bomb that would explode at the end of the Menem period, a decade later.

The combination of these factors meant that Argentina, perhaps more than any other country, suffered the brutal dismantling of a previously powerful state sector – including the state oil company, YPF (Yacimientos Petrolíferos Fiscales), which had ensured the country's self-sufficiency in oil. The government privatized it with a simple vote in Congress.

In this way, one of the most advanced systems of economic and social integration, which linked economic growth to the extension of the domestic consumer market, was torn apart. Both aspects had been weakened by the military dictatorship. Now it was one of the most traditional forces of Latin American nationalism that would complete the implementation of the plan.

In different guises, Peronism had dominated Argentina's history for six decades, displacing the traditional left. By defeating the Socialist and Communist parties, it weakened support for these parties, cut them off from their social base, and left few alternatives for the non-Peronist left. One of these was to ally with the liberal right, based on a critique of Peronism's lack of democracy. A second possibility was to embrace Peronism – which even had a Trotskyist tendency, that of Jorge Abelardo Ramos – and disappear within it. The third alternative was to stay outside, to the left of Peronism, socially isolated, reaffirming doctrinaire principles.

Peronism has adopted contradictory forms over the years, moving from its original nationalism, through López Rega's Triple A (Argentinean Anti-Communist Alliance) during the government of Isabelita Perón,[5] to Menem's neoliberalism and finally the Kirchners.

One consequence of this combination between the role of Peronism, the dictatorship and the crises of hyperinflation – which occurred at the beginning of Menem's mandate, as well as during the previous government of Raúl Alfonsín – is that Argentina has become one of the countries of the region where the left finds it most difficult to project its image and take on a significant role in national politics. The tumultuous

---

5. The Alianza Anticomunista Argentina was a right-wing death-squad operating in the 1970s, mainly during the presidency of Isabel Perón, 1974–1976. It was linked to the Peronist right and targeted radical activists, including those of the Peronist left. After the military coup in 1976, it was largely absorbed into the repressive apparatus of the dictatorship.

relationship between a Kirchnerite left and a wide range of small groups with doctrinaire politics and limited mass support or political influence, does not create an environment in which social movements can easily develop convincing alternatives.

It was left to the organizations of the unemployed, known as the *piqueteros*, and of factory occupations to take the lead in resisting neoliberalism – a situation that was repeated in almost all of Latin America. Social movements, old and new, came to the forefront in the resistance to neoliberal governments, with their programmes of privatizations, rolling back the state economically and socially, opening up the economies and stimulating development based on exports, the consumption of luxury goods and ever more precarious forms of employment. Like the piqueteros in Argentina, so too the Zapatistas in Mexico, the landless in Brazil, and the indigenous movements in Bolivia and Ecuador stood at the head of such resistance. The big trade union organizations, weakened by soaring unemployment and the 'flexibilization' of labour relations, took part in these struggles, but they had lost the central role they had played in the popular struggles of previous decades.

The 1990s, then, were characterized by these neoliberal offensives and the resistance put up by the social movements. Neoliberalism managed to create a consensus around its policies, partly because of strong international propaganda, but also because it was able to play on the spectre of inflation, the single most important issue used in Latin America to criminalize the state and justify sharp fiscal adjustments. The immediate effects of monetary stabilization – and the illusion that this measure, on its own, would substantially raise people's purchasing power and produce a recovery of economic development – was what enabled the re-election of those presidents who had been the standard-bearers of neoliberalism: Menem, Cardoso and Fujimori. Politically, this was the defining characteristic of the 1990s.

In this polarized situation, resistance was centred on the social movements and the strength of their own organization.

These acted as the catalysts of growing popular discontent. But they were limited by their inability to develop a political force that could put forward alternative models, or a political bloc capable of winning elections and putting such models into practice.

The World Social Forums (WSFs) were an expression of this on the international level. They embodied a view that reduced the struggle exclusively to the social movements and NGOs, in explicit opposition to political organizations and to politics itself, privileging a supposed civil society. The protests against the World Trade Organization (WTO) meetings, beginning in Seattle, the campaigns against the war in Iraq, and the holding of the WSFs themselves, were the main manifestations of this form of struggle against neoliberalism. But this first period ran out of steam. Two things revealed its limitations. The first was the struggle against the war in Iraq. The WSF never included the anti-war struggle among its themes because this meant confronting directly political and strategic issues, power relations and imperial policies. Activities around this were always parallel additions, never part of the official programme; as a result, the WSFs disappeared from the world political scene, precisely because this was now dominated by the topic of war, which the United States had imposed. The movement against war and for peace then petered out, but no other struggle took its place. The success of the biggest demonstrations the world has ever seen was not even a subject of debate.

The other main limit was set by the shift from a phase of resistance to one of building alternatives. This shift took place mainly in Latin America, with governments as the key protagonists. All alternatives capable of superseding neoliberalism depend on state policies, whether in terms of guaranteeing and extending rights, regulating financial capital, or building alternative alliances to the WTO – an arena that the WSF refused to deal with, thereby confining itself to the phase of resistance, incapable of relating to the alternatives that in practice were beginning to build another possible world.

CYCLES OF STRUGGLE

In the half century since the victory of the Cuban Revolution in 1959, the continent has lived through several cycles of political struggle, of ups and downs, triumphs and setbacks. Their rise and fall have come in quick succession, compared to the time-spans of the European left. The result has been a series of recalibrations in the balance of power between classes and between social, political or ideological camps. This reflects the prolonged crisis of hegemony that overtook the region when the import-substitution model that had held sway since the crash of 1929 finally ran out of steam.

The first cycle, from 1959 to 1967, saw the triumph of the Cuban revolution and the spread of the rural guerrilla movement to Venezuela, Guatemala and Peru, in emulation of those of Colombia and Nicaragua. There were mass mobilizations in several countries, including Brazil during Goulart's 1961–1964 government and, following the military coup in 1964, struggles of resistance against the dictatorship. For the Latin American left this was a period of upswing, directly influenced by the success of Cuba, but cut short by the death of Che Guevara in Bolivia in 1967. The second cycle runs from 1967 to 1973. It saw the decline of rural guerrilla movements and the rise of new urban guerrillas in Uruguay, Brazil and Argentina. Allende was elected president in Chile (1970–1973); the same years saw the government of Juan José Torres (1971) in Bolivia, and nationalist governments under Juan Velasco Alvarado in Peru (1967) and Omar Torrijos in Panama (1968). In summary, this was a mixed period inaugurating an era of reverses, marked by military coups and dictatorships.

The years 1973 to 1979 saw the consolidation of military dictatorships across the Southern Cone. As in Brazil, juntas came to power in Bolivia in 1971, Chile and Uruguay in 1973 and Argentina in 1976. Velasco Alvarado was overthrown in Peru. The neoliberal model was rolled out in Pinochet's Chile. This was a period of unmitigated downturn. By contrast, the long decade of 1979 to 1990 brought Sandinista victory in

Nicaragua, revolution in Grenada and a nationalist government in Surinam. Castro was elected president of the Movement of Non-Aligned Countries, and guerrilla forces expanded in El Salvador and Guatemala. The 1980s were a period of overall progress.

In another switch, the years from 1990 to 1998 saw the Sandinista defeat, the start of the 'special period' in Cuba, and the entrenchment of neoliberal hegemony across the continent, with the collaboration of the PRI in Mexico, Menem in Argentina, Pérez in Venezuela, Cardoso in Brazil, Fujimori in Peru and the continuation of Pinochetist economic neoliberalism in Chile under the Concertación coalition of Socialists and Christian Democrats. This was definitively a period of net regression. Yet from 1998 onwards, the wind turned in the other direction with the election of Chávez in Venezuela, followed by the launch of the World Social Forums in Porto Alegre in 2001, Lula's election victory in 2002, and further gains for the left and centre-left in Argentina, Uruguay, Bolivia, Nicaragua, Ecuador and finally Paraguay. Mercosur was being expanded to incorporate Venezuela and Bolivia, while the Alianza Bolivariana para los Pueblos de Nuestra América – or ALBA, 'dawn' –brought together a new left grouping of the Andean–Caribbean axis. So far, this has been a period of appreciable progress.

This succession of short ups and downs shows, over the half century, an ascending curve – what we might call a long wave of growing popular struggles. The brevity of each cycle indicates the region's instability and its inability to consolidate alternatives; it shows the depth of the crisis of hegemony and, at the same time, the left's astounding ability to recover from its defeats, no matter how crushing these seem to be – Che's murder, the coup in Chile, the rout of the Sandinistas, the tightening grip of neoliberal processes. Like a mole, the popular movement repressed in one country has popped up elsewhere. It tunnelled from the south to the north of the continent, from the country to the city, from the discourse of the old left to new forms of expression, from party structures to looser social movements, and from these to new political and ideological forces. In other parts of the world, defeats on the scale experienced here led to long periods of abeyance, for example after the loss of Germany and Italy in the wake of the First World War, or the crushing of republicanism after the Spanish Civil War.

The brevity of the cycles is indeed surprising: only three years passed between the death of Che and the ebbing of the first guerrillero wave in 1967, and the election of Allende in 1970. From the 1973 military coups in Chile and Uruguay, and that of 1976 in Argentina, to the 1979 victory of the Sandinistas – six and three years respectively. And from the collapse of the Socialist world and the beginning of the 'special period' in Cuba, preceded by the overthrow of the Grenadan government in 1983 and the end of the Sandinista regime in 1990, it was only eight or nine years until the election of Chávez. The neoliberal model was just beginning to put down roots when its first crisis erupted in Mexico in 1994 – the year that NAFTA was signed and the Zapatista rebellion broke out, while Cardoso was taking office in Brazil. Notably, however, the three progressive cycles together add up to twenty-nine years, encompassing the victory of the Cuban and Nicaraguan revolutions and the governments of Allende, Chávez, Morales and Correa. By contrast, the periods of retreat make up a total of fourteen years, including the death of Che, the Chilean coup and the Sandinista defeat.

CYCLES OF NEOLIBERALISM

Why did Latin America become the laboratory for neoliberal policies, and why, in a rather short period of time, did it then become the weak link in the worldwide neoliberal chain?

From the 1930s, the continent had experienced five decades of continuous economic development. It was a long expansive wave that began with the various responses adopted after the crash of 1929. Those led to the end of the liberal hegemony that held sway in much of Latin America throughout the nineteenth century, and to the decline of the commodity-exporting model that had dominated since colonial times. The main export products might vary – from gold or silver to sugar – but the mechanism was always the same: economies based on the production of often a single commodity, became largely dependent on a single export market. This model collapsed with the crash of 1929 and the contraction of those foreign markets, especially in Britain and the United States, opening the way to a new model that broke with this dependence on primary exports.

Industrialization projects based on import-substitution were implemented in some countries – most intensively in Mexico, Argentina and Brazil, but also more sporadically in Colombia, Peru and Chile. These processes were underwritten by nationalist, political and ideological projects that bolstered the working class, the trade unions and political parties, along with national ideologies and identities in general.

The potential this built up burst onto the political scene in the 1960s as a radical force when the long cycle of growth petered out in conflicts over workers' rights, at a time when the Cuban example was pointing towards alternatives that transcended the limits of capitalism and US imperial domination. The response to these struggles was an era of military coups, first in Brazil and Bolivia in 1964, in Argentina in 1966 and 1976, and finally in Uruguay and Chile in 1973.

The combined and closely related processes of military dictatorship and the application of neoliberal models acted together to yield an extreme regression in the balance of power between social classes. It would have been impossible to carry out the wholesale sell-offs of public assets and national resources that unfolded most drastically in Chile, Uruguay and Argentina without first crushing the people's ability to defend their interests. These three countries had some of the most developed systems of social security anywhere, under states that were capable of regulating and stimulating the domestic market, promoting economic development, guaranteeing social rights and ensuring service delivery. The most brutal repression they had ever known was needed to clear the way for neoliberal policies that privatized state functions – in the case of Argentina, transferring virtually all public resources into the hands of private capital – and abolished hard-won social rights. In short, three of the most enlightened states on the continent found themselves completely dismantled.

By the 1990s, neoliberalism had spread across Latin America as in no other part of the world. The programme was originally implemented by the far right in Pinochet's Chile. It found other right-wing adepts, such as Alberto Fujimori in Peru, but also absorbed forces that had historically been associated with nationalism: the PRI in Mexico; Peronism in Argentina under Carlos Menem; in Bolivia, the Nationalist Revolutionary Movement – the party that had headed the nationalist revolution of 1952 under Víctor Paz Estenssoro. After this, neoliberalism moved on to social democracy, gaining the adherence of the Chilean Socialist Party, Venezuela's Acción Democrática, and the Brazilian Social-Democratic Party. It became a hegemonic system across almost the entire territory of Latin America and penetrated almost all of the political spectrum.

Nevertheless, the neoliberal model failed to consolidate the social forces necessary for its stabilization, resulting in the early onset of crises that would check its course. Deregulation, designed to remove all obstacles to the free flow of capital, led – as we now know only too clearly – to vast resources being channelled not into production but into finance, where capital could obtain higher returns, with greater liquidity and almost always tax-free. Along with the rapid opening up of the economies, this produced not only an intense concentration of income, loss of formal employment rights for workers and rising unemployment, but also the de-industrialization of much of the continent.

As a result, once the initial, positive impact of monetary stabilization had passed, these neoliberal governments could not consolidate a solid bloc of classes to support them. They produced extreme fragmentation among the middle classes, co-opting some of its more privileged layers to support the process of economic modernization, while pushing the majority further into poverty; at the same time, they managed to neutralize some of the reaction of the masses by using unemployment and informal employment to divide them. Thus the model passed, rather quickly, from euphoria to depression, and to the isolation of the governments that promoted it. The three largest Latin American economies were the theatre for the most dramatic crises. In Mexico in 1994, Brazil in 1999 and Argentina in 2002, the programme crumbled without delivering on its promises. The ravages of hyper-inflation were checked, but this was only achieved at a tremendous cost. For a decade or more, economic development was paralysed, the concentration of wealth grew greater than ever, public deficits spiralled and the mass of the population had their rights expropriated, most notably in the domain of employment and labour relations. On top of this, national debt expanded exponentially and regional economies became highly vulnerable, helplessly exposed to attack from speculators, as these three countries each discovered to their cost.

However, neoliberalism's biggest achievements were not in the economic field, where most of its promise had lain, but in the social and ideological fields. The combination of flexible labour-market policies (meaning a 'precarious' labour market, where the right to a formal employment contract had been taken away), unemployment resulting from cuts in public spending, and massive lay-offs in the private sector, gravely weakened trade unions and the workers' ability to negotiate; the workforce found itself fragmented and atomized, while labour issues and working conditions disappeared from public debate. The majority of Latin Americans can no longer organize, have no recourse to justice and no public identity. They are hardly really citizens, because they exercise no real rights and are the victims of the worst kinds of super-exploitation. They are the so-called 'excluded', not in the sense that they are marginalized from existing social processes, but because they have no right of redress, that is, they are not recognized by the labour market: their basic social rights have been taken away.

In addition to this social fragmentation, which makes resistance more difficult, there have been radical ideological changes in Latin American societies. The defeat of the socialist camp internationally was followed by an ideological project that replaced many key points of reference: the state by the private firm and the market place, the citizen by the consumer, economic regulation by free trade, public spaces by shopping malls, the worker by the individual, ideology by marketing, the word by the image, writing by visual media and the book by the video, street rallies by political campaigns on TV, rights by competition, the printed novel by the soap opera, and newspapers by TV news bulletins. In other words, we saw the consolidation of ideological values that had been gaining in importance for some time and that found their fullest expression in the ideological milieu of triumphant neoliberalism.

Hand in hand with the affirmation of this set of values went the dismissal of another set of values, phenomena and spaces: parties, politics, collective solutions, state planning, rights, theories, ideology, values, reason, social conscience, social movements and organizations, the public sphere and the business of state.

Added to this were the campaigns on behalf of the 'single orthodoxy' and the 'Washington Consensus', that aimed to shape a prevailing intellectual landscape unquestioningly favourable to capitalism in its neoliberal phase. This, as well as the social fragmentation mentioned before, became one of the main pillars of the neoliberal order and largely explains why it has remained hegemonic in Latin America to this day, even though its economic achievements were short-lived and many of the governments that personified it were defeated: Alberto Fujimori in Peru, Fernando Henrique Cardoso in Brazil, Carlos Menem in Argentina, Carlos Andrés Pérez in Venezuela, Gonzalo Sánchez de Lozada in Bolivia, the last PRI governments in Mexico, governments of the two traditional parties in Uruguay and the Colorado Party in Paraguay. The same goes for the defeat of those who tried to continue the model even after it had failed, and who fell as a result, like

Fernando de la Rúa in Argentina, Lucio Gutiérrez in Ecuador, and others. More than ten governments in the region were toppled, not this time by military coups, but by their own loss of legitimacy.

POST-NEOLIBERALISM IN LATIN AMERICA

Two big changes have occurred in the world in the current historical period: one is the shift from a bipolar world to a unipolar one, under the imperial hegemony of the United States; the second is the substitution of the neoliberal model for the previous, regulated model. This combination produced a regression of historic proportions, with very negative changes in the balance of power between the basic political camps on both local and international levels.

After the confrontation between these two camps, the socialist and the capitalist, the victory of the latter inaugurated a new historical period, under the leadership of a single leading power. This was an economic and political victory, but also an ideological one. During the bipolar period, the interpretation of modern history was in dispute. For the socialist camp, the chief conflict in the world was between socialism and capitalism, with the capitalist model expected to disappear. For the capitalist camp, it was between democracy and totalitarianism: with the Nazi version of the latter defeated, the struggle against its communist version came to the fore.

The end of the socialist camp and the triumph of its enemies was also a victory for their world view. What now prevailed was the vision expressed by Francis Fukuyama, who saw contemporary history as confined to liberal democracy – which was now identified with democracy *per se* – and to the capitalist market economy – identified with the economy *tout court*. It was an extraordinary ideological victory, which reasserted on the level of ideas the changes already introduced in practice.

It is on this level that US hegemony displays its greatest asset: the notion of the 'North-American way of life', which exerts a profound influence, even on the poorest sections of the world's population, or on China – which had never before experienced significant foreign influence.

Nonetheless, the economic, political and military weaknesses of the United States affect its capacity to exert hegemony. Militarily and politically, it is unable to conduct two wars at the same time; this limits its ability to assert itself as the single super-power, the great world leader in the age of globalization. The recession in the United States has confirmed these weaknesses, which are reflected in the devaluation of the dollar and the three structural deficits that have come to characterize the US economy.

The new, unipolar, imperial hegemony did not emerge in a period of capitalist expansion and has been unable to generate a new cycle of growth, like that of the post-Second-World-War boom. The dominance of finance capital has made speculation the main area of accumulation, attracting massive surpluses of capital. This is a consequence of the structural contradiction between expanded production and the inability of the system to create the conditions for its realization through similarly expanded consumption. The relative decline of the United States' economic hegemony and the rise of Asian economies – principally China – also reflect this tendency.

The ideological factors mentioned earlier make it difficult to accept the idea that there could be domination without hegemony.[6] The United States' ideological influence is, on the contrary, a classic case of hegemony in the Gramscian sense, implying an ability to convince, persuade, fascinate, seduce and induce the adoption of North American life-style values. For the world's poor, the symptoms of this induction into North American values include the obsession with consuming brandname products like McDonald's, the internet and, in the case of China, with the use of cars and technology.

No other way of life competes with the North American in the hearts and imaginations of most of the world's population.

---

6. See, in particular, Giovanni Arrighi. The concept is more widespread, however, being taken up by such excellent analysts as Immanuel Wallerstein and Samir Amin.

Neither Islamism, nor Evangelism, nor any other alternative, Western or otherwise, can come close to competing with the lifestyle, values and consumer habits of the North Americans. Another powerful factor favouring the continued, albeit weakened, hegemony of the US is the fact that no other country or alliance of countries has the political, military, economic or ideological power to challenge the US's position.

At the same time, however, the neoliberal model reveals its limitations. As was to be expected, the country that derived most benefit from financial deregulation ended up as its victim. This is what has now happened to the United States, obliged to bail out financial companies in crisis. Various forms of state intervention and protectionism – which had managed to survive – have grown stronger, without putting into question the fundamental theories of free trade which continue to dominate the world.

In terms of both political and military hegemony, as well as in terms of the hegemony of the neoliberal model itself – now in decline – there is no new power on the horizon in a position to exert hegemony itself nor with an alternative to the neoliberal model. We therefore live, and will continue to live for a good while yet, in a historical period marked by turbulence, uncertainty and fresh hegemonic disputes, both economically and in the political and military domains.

This hiatus exists because the greatest drama of our time lies in this mismatch between, on the one hand, an ever clearer revelation of the limitations of capitalism – through the financialization of the economy, the militarization of conflicts, the environmental degradation and the concentration of wealth and power within each country and worldwide – and, on the other, the retreat of those factors that could help to build an alternative to replace capitalism. This is not only down to the defeat and disappearance of the USSR and the socialist camp, it is also a function of the changes within capitalism itself. These include the weakening of the working class – both its objective situation and the importance attributed to labour – as well as the weakening of all kinds of public policy and state regulation, of collective alternatives, of politics as an instrument for consciously changing society, and of ideology and political activism, among other things.

In this new historical period, counter-hegemonic alternatives confront the two main pillars of the dominant system: the neoliberal model and US imperial hegemony. And it is in this confrontation that we must measure the process of building 'another possible world', in order to judge its real advances and setbacks, obstacles and possibilities.

To a certain degree, we can divide the main axes of power in the world today into to three great monopolies: of arms, of money, and of words. The first reflects the militarization of conflicts, an area in which the United States believes it exercises unquestionable superiority. The second relates to neoliberal policy, the commercialization of all social relations and natural resources, which seeks to create a world in which everything has its price, everything can be bought and sold, and whose utopia is the shopping mall. The third has to do with the monopoly of the private media over the profoundly selective and anti-democratic process of shaping public opinion. Latin America mirrors in a peculiar way these contradictions of the new historical period. Just as it was the stage for first introducing the neoliberal model, and later became its privileged victim, so the region is going through a certain neoliberal hangover, with some governments that break with the model and others that try to tweak it in order not to be brought down with it. Politically, the region proved unreceptive to Washington's policy of 'infinite war': the United States didn't get the support of any government for its invasion of Iraq. Within the region, Colombia, as the regional epicentre of US policy, has remained isolated. Overall, the region has developed areas of relative autonomy from the economic and political hegemony of the United States, which makes Latin America the weakest link in the neoliberal chain at the beginning of this new century.

It is in this framework that the new historical period in Latin America has been fashioned, both as a result of and as a reaction to the prevailing conditions in the world. The decline of the economic model was a decisive factor in the defeat of the governments that introduced and implemented it in the continent, and for the weakness of those that still maintained it – like Felipe Calderón in Mexico and Alan García in Peru, both with clearly declining popularity, and Michelle Bachelet in Chile. Since then, Chile's Concertación has suffered a serious defeat by the neo-Pinochetist candidate, Sebastián Piñera, which has deepened the crisis within the opposition, leading to new divisions and preparing the way for the right to continue in power.

In Colombia, Álvaro Uribe, whose considerable popularity derived from his promotion of 'democratic security' – the key question in that country – did manage to get his chosen successor, Juan Manuel Santos, elected. But he soon saw his protégé distance himself from some of the key policies.

More and more presidents were elected, and some of them re-elected, as a reaction to the exhaustion of the economic model. Added to this was the isolation of the Bush administration, with its defeat over the FTAA and its recourse to bilateral free-trade treaties as an alternative. Along with the strength accumulated by the social movements in their resistance to neoliberal administrations, these new governments were the driving factor for this new period in Latin America.

2

The Crisis of Hegemony in Latin America

Latin America has lived through clearly distinct historical periods in recent decades. The shifts between them have provoked the deep and permanent instability, both political and social, that characterizes our epoch.

THE DEVELOPMENTALIST MODEL

The reaction to the crash of 1929 involved promoting, in different ways and to different degrees, industrial development, the internal market and the development of national projects. This period, which began in the 1930s, continued through to the end of the long postwar boom and produced one major historical novelty. Up until then, the capitalist periphery had been condemned to exporting primary commodities, while industrialization remained the exclusive reserve of the central capitalist countries. International trade theory took upon itself the task of theorizing and justifying this particular international division of labour, inherited from the colonial era.

It is possible to identify three groups of countries, according to how they reacted to the Great Depression after 1929:

those that succeeded in introducing industrialization projects to substitute for imports, thereby transforming the country's productive apparatus (Argentina, Mexico and Brazil); those that took some steps in this direction (Peru, Chile, Uruguay and Colombia); and those that remained trapped in the commodity-exporting model. Nonetheless, however much the first two groups might benefit from the 'privilege of backwardness' deriving from the law of uneven and combined development, such belated industrialization came up against an already existing world market, with which it had to come to terms in order to be integrated into it.

The dependent forms of peripheral industrialization were duly analysed by Ruy Mauro Marini,[1] who pointed to accumulation directed at exports and at high-end consumption, based on the super-exploitation of labour, and to the social consequences which only deepened existing inequalities in the most unequal, and therefore the most unjust, continent in the world.

Latin America changed in a way unprecedented in its history, whether in terms of the development of its productive forces, the shaping of its basic social classes (aided by greater state regulation, welfare provision, and intervention to stimulate production), or the elaboration of national projects (through organizing social and political forces and creating cultural identities). There was upwards social mobility, especially from the primary sector (agriculture and mining) to the secondary and tertiary sectors (industry and services), which implied acquiring a formal contract of employment and full citizenship. This was how a large urban proletariat was formed, expanding the trade unions, strengthening political parties of a popular character and developing a culture of citizenship, rights and democracy, in spite of the deep social inequalities.

---

1. See Emir Sader (ed.), *Dialética da dependência: uma antologia da obra de Ruy Mauro Marini*, Petrópolis 2000. Ruy Mauro Marini, 1932–1997, was a Brazilian Marxist activist and academic who spent many years in exile in Chile and Mexico and had considerable influence among the Latin American left during the 1970s and 1980s. He developed a radical, Marxist version of dependency theory, and introduced the notion of 'sub-imperialism' to describe the role of Brazil's military regime after 1965.

At the end of this long cycle of Latin American growth, stability gave way to big social and political upheavals, including military dictatorships, guerrilla movements and revolutionary victories. Underneath all this, it was the end of that cycle of developmentalism, state regulation and expansion of the domestic market for mass consumption; of nationalist movements and alliances between sectors of the industrial bourgeoisie and forces representing the workers and the left.

It was the end of a period dominated by a bloc of classes that had acquired a certain stability. This domination was based on a project of capital accumulation, which incorporated shared interests in the expansion of domestic consumption, the increased integration of workers into the formal economy, the strengthening of the role of the state and, to some extent, the promotion of economic development and defence of the domestic market.

NEOLIBERAL HEGEMONY

Once this project was dead and buried, and after a tense period of transition, the neoliberal model was enthroned in a world dominated by US imperial hegemony. Deregulation – the strategic concept of this new phase – did not produce a new cycle of growth, but rather a brutal and massive transfer of capital from the productive to the speculative spheres. Freed of constraints, capital migrated en masse to the financial sector through the purchase of public debt and stock-market movements.

Simultaneously there was a weakening of the regulatory capacity of states and a scaling back of social policies – as a result of growing debts and the letters of intent imposed by the International Monetary Fund (IMF) – alongside the privatization of public assets and the opening up of the economies internationally.

A new power bloc was installed, led by finance capital, which was now allied to big groups of exporters and gave a new importance to agribusiness, especially soybean cultivation. The weak point of this alliance was the difficulty it had in winning and sustaining popular support. The new bloc managed to draw in sections of the upper middle class already implicated in the processes of economic globalization. But this left the middle classes deeply divided, with the more traditional sectors increasingly proletarianized.

The new model was launched with great fanfare. It enjoyed international support and the virtually unanimous backing of the private media. It was acclaimed as the great instrument of financial stability, capable of purging the public coffers and promoting a new cycle of economic modernization and growth. Inflation was brought under control at the cost of an astronomic increase in the public debt and very high interest rates; financial stability replaced economic development as the underlying objective, and this in a continent still bedevilled by unresolved economic and social problems.

After a brief period of euphoria at its success in controlling inflation, there began a series of crises that revealed the new model's limited ability to reproduce the conditions of its own existence: Mexico in 1994, Brazil in 1999, Argentina in 2001 and 2002. The opening up of the economies, together with the structural dependence on speculative capital, produced weaknesses that triggered these crises and revealed the fragility of neoliberalism before it could deliver on its promises of renewed economic growth, modernization and widened access to consumption.

Why did this happen, if the West, under the unquestioned leadership of the United States, had triumphed in the Cold War while the opposing camp – bearer of a different social project and world view – had disappeared? Why did this happen, if the transition from regulation to the free market had been almost universal, with support from right across the political and ideological spectrum?

The central factor was that, underlying the critique of the regulatory role of the state, which placed constraints on the free realization of capital, was the thesis of free circulation, which genuinely believed that 'the market is the best means of allocating resources'. In practice this meant a massive transfer of resources from production into speculation. As a structural feature of the period of capital surpluses, this not only blocked any possibility of a new long wave of economic growth, but also ensured the supremacy of finance capital in its speculative form.

Financial accumulation, in turn, does not create the social support base it requires for its own stable reproduction. This is its Achilles heel. The reproduction of fictitious capital does not distribute income. On the contrary, it accentuates the concentration of income, because its turnover is imaginary, creating neither value nor jobs.

It was no accident that, after a euphoric beginning, the governments which adhered most closely to the neoliberal model were defeated at the ballot box, and those that replaced them put social policies at the centre of their platforms. This lent them legitimacy and allowed them to defeat the right, even though the latter had a monopoly of the media and could therefore encourage and manipulate public opinion on behalf of the opposition. Power relations remained dramatically transformed, with new concentrations of power in the monopolies connected with land – now mainly agribusiness for export – and also with banking, the media and the larger industrial and commercial corporations.

Yet even the unity of all these sectors of big capital, led by finance capital, has proved unable to forge a broad base of support, in spite of the alliance with new, globalized sectors of the middle class – which were, in any case, a minority among the middle layers. In spite of the role the big commercial media came to play as political and ideological leaders of the new Latin American right, their ability to mobilize and consolidate political support is limited, despite the immense ideological influence they exercise.

In fact, the greatest victory for the new neoliberal right had to do precisely with this media influence, linked up with big-brand marketing campaigns and shopping-mall consumerism – the necessary complement for all of these being television itself and the whole new image industry. Nonetheless, what most contributed to neoliberal hegemony was the immense social and cultural fragmentation that the new model produced and reproduced in broad swathes of the population. Such fragmentation makes it more difficult to demonstrate, to negotiate, to appeal to the courts and to build a political party, just as it weakens people's own identification with the world of labour and with working-class culture.

Another aspect of neoliberal hegemony, one we want to emphasize because of its importance, is alienation. It is a concept that has rather fallen into disuse, but which today, more than in any other period of history, plays a crucial role. The very loss of working-class identity makes it more difficult to grasp the centrality of the biggest alienation of all: people produce the world, but do not decide the course it takes and are not even aware that they are producing it. On the contrary, they experience it as *ancho y ajeno*, 'a wide and alien world'. This makes it easier to corral people, who have few defences, behind the ideology of globalization, which exalts technology, individual competitiveness, money and managerial skills as the great agents of wealth creation.

This empty space created by the operations of globalization is filled with ideologies of consumerism, the market and competition, which feed the soul and increase demand. The 'North American way of life' was never so developed, never had so much influence, never exercised its hegemony so broadly.

As a result of that convergence, humanity has accumulated an unprecedented technological capacity to build 'another world', in the image and likeness of its dreams, desires and imaginings. However, never before has it felt so impotent before this world, which appears as a reality that is imposed, inevitable, unavoidable, utterly foreign to what men and women really experience in their daily lives, or in their daily struggles.

Neoliberalism has had other effects too. For example, it turned the issue of fighting inflation into a point of universal consensus – so much so that many governments elected in a demonstration of opposition to the model (Brazil, Argentina, Uruguay and others) held on to various of its elements such as the independence of the Central Bank, the emphasis on ensuring a primary surplus to pay the debt, accumulation of large foreign reserves and high interest rates.

When international capital moved into a long recessive cycle, for Latin America this represented much more than just a change of economic direction. Starting in the 1970s, the continent moved into a period historically overdetermined by a twofold shift, from a bipolar world to one of unipolar, imperialist hegemony, and from the regulated model to the neoliberal one. This combination deepened the split between the centre and the periphery – now referred to as the relation between globalizers and globalized.

THE CRISIS OF HEGEMONY

Latin America was the laboratory of neoliberalism. Here it was born, here it spread and here it took on its most radical forms. As a result, the continent suffered a neoliberal hangover and became the weakest link in this chain, with a proliferation of governments elected on the back of opposition to neoliberalism, contrary to the tendency elsewhere in the world.

In other moments of history, when the period was different, shorter and less severe social crises have elicited mass responses from social movements; due to the fragmentation caused by neoliberalism, these have become the exception. In the current period, social discontent is channelled elsewhere: into religion, or into private or public violence, amongst other things, as if the energy in society were denied any kind of political development, but were, on the contrary, neutralized.

This period is characterized by a loss of legitimacy on the part of both governments and neoliberal policies, but also by difficulties in developing alternatives, either because of the social fragmentation already mentioned, or because of the conservative consensus that continues to uphold free trade around the world, or because of the legacy of the neoliberal consensus itself. This left its mark not only on social attitudes, like the fear of inflation, but also on economic processes, in spite of the very real risk of monetary chaos caused by the imbalance between production and consumption. The latter was, in turn, a result of the regressive income distribution caused by neoliberal policies.

Another barrier to developing alternatives is the fact that these governments remained locked in a struggle for hegemony with the big bourgeoisie and its enduring centres of power – large private companies, national and foreign, banks, export-oriented agribusiness, private media conglomerates. Even if this elite no longer enjoyed broad support at home, it could still count on powerful, international allies, especially among the 'globalizing' countries.

In these countries, a rightist drift has swept the political landscape in recent decades, based on an ever greater concentration of wealth and power – never before has the gap in living standards between the centre and the periphery of capitalism been so great. If one explanation for the spread of welfare states after the Second World War lay in the need to improve the living standards of people in Western Europe, in view of the competition and possible threat from the socialist countries, this had now disappeared. It swept away with it the political space occupied by the communist parties, and by the same token ended the traditional alliance that had sustained the left throughout that period – between the social democrats and the communists.

From the social point of view, while trade unions grew weaker as full employment gave way to high levels of unemployment, the arrival of immigrants to take up unskilled jobs allowed some on the right to manipulate the unemployed and turn them against the immigrants, thereby boosting their share of the vote and often winning majorities. Immigration policy continued to be the dividing line between right and left, even as new and tougher restrictions on the entry and legal status of immigrants were approved by almost all shades of the political spectrum. At the same time, these economies went into recession and working hours increased again, sometimes reaching seventy hours a week or more.

One thing is certain: never has the South been so isolated from the North. The latter, led by the North Americans, acts in a concerted manner to defend its interests, bringing together all of Western Europe, most of Eastern Europe, Japan, and, of course, the United States. The South began again to build its own organizations, to play a bigger part in forums like the G20, to sign agreements and deals, to fight for its rights in the Doha Round of trade talks and to resist the indiscriminate opening up of its markets to the powers of the North; but it does all this as the South, unable to count on any allies at the centre of the system, which remains united as a dominant bloc in defence of its own interests.

The future of Latin America in the first half of the twenty-first century depends on the fate of those governments that are currently promoting regional integration, resisting US free trade policies, and either advancing towards a post-neoliberal model, or at least reworking it with the introduction of social policies that espouse a different logic.

NEW DIRECTIONS IN LATIN AMERICA

The present historical moment for Latin America is, then, one of hegemonic crisis: neoliberalism and the bloc of forces supporting it have run out of steam, and only survive in so far as the model is applied in a qualified form (as in the cases of Brazil, Argentina and Uruguay); at the same time the construction of an alternative model, and a new bloc of forces, faces huge obstacles. We talk of 'post-neoliberalism', but this is a descriptive category that refers to varying degrees of rejection of the model, not yet to a new model; at the same time, the alliances supporting these new projects are made up of a widely varying patchwork of forces.

Hence the instability of these governments, which have advanced along the lines of least resistance in the neoliberal chain – especially social policy and regional integration

– following the retreat of those who applied the model in its orthodox form, but which have begun to meet stiffer resistance as the right-wing opposition, led ideologically and even politically by the private media, has regrouped. This conflict is set to shape Latin America, not just through the second decade of the twenty-first century, but through the whole first half of this century.

What would be the most favourable international context for the reinforcement, and perhaps extension, of these governments? To what extent does, or could, their development draw on favourable international circumstances?

Neoliberal hegemony went through three phases internationally, corresponding to its rise, consolidation and crisis, and reflecting the main currents in government in the central capitalist countries. Its rise was symbolized by the Thatcher–Reagan partnership, when its ideological expression was at its most virulent, openly conservative and restorationist; the Pinochet regime was its purest expression, and the carnage wreaked on the Bolivian mining sector by the ideas of neoliberal guru, Jeffrey Sachs, showed just how far the new model was prepared to go to impose its recipes and its hegemony.

The second phase corresponded to the governments of the so-called 'third way', personified by Bill Clinton and Tony Blair, who succeeded the other duo in the Anglo-Saxon world and applied a supposedly 'light' version of neoliberalism. However, the heavy lifting – the privatizations, unbridling of markets and dismantlement of trade barriers – had already been done. It was in this phase that neoliberalism showed the breadth of its power in the capitalist heartlands, with the adhesion of social democratic governments. To some extent this shift had been anticipated in the 1980s by François Mitterrand and Felipe González; but in the 1990s, followers emerged in almost all European countries, including Germany, Portugal and Italy, closing a circle that now encompassed all the most important governments of the region. Social democracy made a comeback, this time as the standard-bearer of globalization.

It was as if a green light had been given for like-minded

governments around the world – social democrats and nationalists – to follow suit. Salinas de Gortari and Carlos Menem, both from traditional currents of Latin American nationalism, joined the Bolivian MNR, represented by the governments of Paz Estenssoro and Sánchez de Lozada. The adhesion of European social democracy, especially in Spain and France, where the links with similar currents in Latin America were stronger, opened the season for enrolments over here: after the Chilean socialists – in alliance with the Christian Democrats – there followed the governments of Fernando Henrique Cardoso in Brazil, Carlos Andrés Pérez in Venezuela, and Alberto Fujimori and Alejandro Toledo in Peru, to name just a few.

That was the most propitious moment for the spread of neoliberal governments, because it combined a (short) expansive cycle in the US economy, through the so-called 'new economy', with governments that saw themselves as a 'second wave', to use Perry Anderson's expression.[2] This seemed to confirm the 'Washington Consensus' and the 'single orthodoxy', which brought together behind the same model a range of currents with such varied histories as those represented by Pinochet, Salinas de Gortari and Fernando Henrique Cardoso. The association with the 'third way' served as a justification for those governments previously identified with social welfare policies to fall in behind a strict neoliberal model. Countries like Brazil and Venezuela, which had never lived through the hard phase of neoliberalism, of the sort experienced by the United States and Britain under Reagan and Thatcher, signed up to a thinking which in theory sought a middle course between the market and the state.

It was not by chance that the combination of economic growth in the United States – which in the 1990s still weighed very heavily in Latin America's international economic relations – with this 'third way' formula was what most favoured the spread of neoliberal governments. Always with the exception of Cuba.

2. Perry Anderson, 'Testing Formula Two', *New Left Review* 8, March–April 2001.

The third phase, at the very end of the 1990s, corresponds to the decline of the illusion that a 'new economy' would ensure smooth and continuous growth. Crises of globalized capitalism, the end of the growth cycle and the rise to power of George W. Bush – who adopted a harsher tone in his command of the imperialist bloc, aided and abetted by the very same Tony Blair – as well as the atmosphere generated by the attacks of 11 September 2001, all led to a conservative turn. Once again, the signs were reversed: Washington adopted belligerent policies and the economy stagnated. To this picture should be added the modernization and exponential growth of the Chinese economy, and the links China promptly developed with some Latin American countries, helping decisively to reduce the importance of trade with the United States.

This framework encouraged a surprising multiplication of governments that favoured regional integration, defeating those that had occupied the stage during the last decade of the twentieth century. Carlos Andrés Pérez and Rafael Caldera were replaced by Hugo Chávez in Venezuela, Fernando Henrique Cardoso by Luiz Inácio Lula da Silva in Brazil, the Blanco and Colorado governments by Tabaré Vázquez in Uruguay, Sánchez de Lozada by Evo Morales in Bolivia, Lucio Gutiérrez by Rafael Correa in Ecuador, and Nicanor Duarte and the Colorado Party by Fernando Lugo in Paraguay. These governments were both the product of a weakening of US political and economic leadership in Latin America, along with its free trade policies, and the expression of a new bloc of forces. They took advantage of the situation to reject the Free Trade Area of the Americas (FTAA) and put alternative policies in place.

Towards the end of the first decade of this century, when some governments in the region were finding it difficult to continue along their chosen course, especially in Venezuela, Bolivia and Argentina, the overall situation began to change. For one thing, the US recession had effects throughout the world economy. Secondly, the election of Barack Obama and the return of a Democrat administration in the United States introduced a new set of political and economic factors on the international stage.

Unlike the 1990s, this time the Democrats would not be able to surf euphorically on a booming economy. Now Washington would have to speak in a different tone if it wanted to overcome its isolation in this region that it had dominated for so long, but where it was now weaker than ever before. These changes, along with the particular problems faced by several of the region's governments, represented a new challenge for regional integration and the development of post-neoliberal alternatives.

Two contrasting scenarios seemed to be possible in this new situation. Either the United States, leaning on its traditional allies – Colombia and Mexico, now joined by Alan García's Peru, which had just signed a free trade agreement with the US – would recover its capacity for co-option, and, adopting a more flexible approach, try to draw towards it the more moderate countries of the regional integration bloc, like Brazil, Argentina and the already predisposed Uruguay, in an attempt to isolate Venezuela, Bolivia, Ecuador and Cuba. Alternatively, the integration projects under way – Mercosur, ALBA, UNASUR, Bank of the South, gas pipelines and so on – would forge ahead, while recession in the north accelerated the diversification of the region's trade with countries like China and made it easier to consolidate these governments and their plans for integration.

It still wasn't clear exactly what would emerge from this combination of recession and Democrat administration, an administration which could not this time rely on a bevy of regional governments enthusiastically supporting its neoliberal policies.

The new US government had to deal with an increasingly integrated South America, whose leaders enjoyed sufficient popular support either to win re-election – as in Bolivia, Venezuela and Ecuador – or to ensure the election of their chosen successors, as in Argentina, Brazil and Uruguay. This gave the United States less room to manoeuvre. At the same time the economic crisis discouraged any closer economic relationship with the United States, like that embodied in the North American Free Trade Agreement and other free trade treaties. Even countries like Peru and Chile, which signed their own free trade agreements with the US, now do more business with China and the Mercosur countries than with the United States.

3

The Lula Enigma

The government of Luiz Inácio Lula da Silva has incurred wildly contradictory judgements: supreme administrator of neoliberalism, according to one left critique; state populist, according to the biggest campaign that the right and the private media giants had ever mounted in this country. Although he carried out social policies that obtained more popular support than any other government has ever won – even in the final stages of his second term he enjoyed 87 per cent support, while his predecessor enjoyed just 18 per cent – Lula was regularly attacked by the radical left, at home and abroad, for not breaking with the economic model he inherited. Some lent him critical support; others attacked head-on. For the former, he represented the moderate left; for the latter, he was a traitor who was to be treated as the main enemy.

What was the nature of Lula's government? The failure to answer this enigma has condemned the right to defeat after defeat, while it has meant that the left – from the most radical to the most moderate – has been unable to develop; unable also to stem a galloping process of depoliticization, or to position itself adequately in relation to the social and political polarization that Brazil is experiencing. With the electoral victory of Lula's chosen successor, Dilma Rousseff, in October 2010, it would seem that the model of government he established is set to be consolidated. All the more important, then, to seek to understand the meaning of Lula's eight-year period in office, both with regard to Brazil's political history and the future it may herald.

LULA AND THE BRAZILIAN LEFT

Any assessment of Lula's record in power must start from an analysis of the origins and context of the Partido dos Trabalhadores's formation. Until a few decades ago, Brazil's left forces were relatively weak in comparison to those of other countries in the region. Their special place on the present world stage is due to a combination of factors which have given the country what Trotsky called the 'privilege of backwardness'. This trajectory is essential to any understanding of the significance of the PT's rise to power, as well as of its limits and contradictions.

Brazil's military coup of 1964 took place earlier than those of Latin American countries where the left was stronger, such as Chile, Argentina or Uruguay. Here the fragility of popular opposition, combined with firm support for the Army from the US – with its strategic interests in Brazil's natural resources – meant that the generals were able to topple the government of João Goulart with a lesser degree of repression than was later required in the Southern Cone. The judiciary and Congress were untouched by the dictatorship, but the unions were closed down and the left was hit hard – making plain the class character of the coup. The final years of the long postwar boom, and an influx of Eurodollars, enabled the military regime to preside over economic expansion from 1967 to 1973, with annual growth rates of over 10 per cent; thanks to a rigid wage policy and foreign capital, growth continued at 7 per cent even after the world economy entered recession. But overseas capital increasingly came to Brazil not as investment, but in the form of loans at fluctuating rates of interest – a time bomb that was to explode after 1979 with the global rise in interest rates.

The dictatorship terminated the historic period of Communist hegemony over the Brazilian left. Both the Partido Comunista Brasileiro (PCB) and the union leaderships allied to it were blamed for the impasse of the mid-twentieth-century popular movement and the failures of resistance to the coup. But the economic expansion of the late 1960s and early '70s brought about a shift in the composition of the labour force, laying the basis for the emergence of a new left movement. Much as in Argentina, injections of foreign – above all North American – capital had led to the establishment of an automobile industry centred on São Paulo. Meanwhile, in the wake of severe droughts on the *sertão*, hundreds of thousands of north-easterners gravitated to the south-central region, and especially metropolitan São Paulo, now the country's economic and financial centre.

Since the regime's economic model was based on exports and the luxury-goods sector, much of the growth of the late 1960s was concentrated in automobile and domestic appliance manufacturing – which in turn increased the weight of working-class fractions in the 'ABC' industrial zone, consisting of the districts of São André, São Bernardo and São Caetano do Sul, on the periphery of São Paulo. It was here that a grass-roots trade unionism developed during the 1970s, despite the military ban, and at the end of the decade – under the leadership of a new generation of trade unionists, including the north-easterner and former car worker Lula – carried out a series of strikes that broke the regime's wage policy.

The PT, founded in 1980, grew principally from a base in this new trade unionism, as activists in São Paulo's automobile industry were joined by unionists from the oil and banking sectors, and by a range of social movements – women's groups, ecologists, indigenous peoples, Afro-Brazilians – and former militants from the armed struggle of the 1960s. The Catholic Church also played a key role, in community organizing inspired by liberation theology. Initially confined to São Paulo, the PT extended its influence into the countryside through the activities of the two largest social movements linked to it, the landless peasants' movement Movimento Sem Terra (MST) and the Central Única dos Trabalhadores (CUT, the more dynamic and radical of the country's two major labour federations). Its heterogeneous origins notwithstanding, the party's ideological identity was from the outset largely conditioned by the outlook of its Paulista trade-union core. This cohort had been educated politically by the struggle against the dictatorship, with the repressive guise in which the state primarily appeared to them informing their anti-statist line. (Brazilian trade unionists had also criticized the state in the past – notably after Vargas's introduction in 1943 of a corporatist Labour Code, borrowed from Mussolini's Italy, which blocked off union autonomy.) Indeed, the new union leaders had less antagonistic relations with the business groups with which they conducted negotiations – often broken up by police raids, after tip-offs from the entrepreneurs themselves – than they did with the state, whose rigid national security doctrine labelled the strike movement as 'subversive'.

Liberal ideology grew to dominate the opposition to the dictatorship after the defeat of armed resistance movements in the late 1960s. A leading role was played by the legal opposition party, the MDB (Movimento Democrático Brasileiro),[1] flanked by social and civil movements and NGOs of a liberal-democratic stamp. The ideology of this oppositional front was provided by the theory of authoritarianism, in the version propounded by Fernando Henrique Cardoso. Common to all these elements was a strong anti-state sentiment, founded on the concept of an antagonism between state and civil society. It was in this period that the Brazilian left began seriously to address the question of democracy, previously marginalized by the PCB in favour of national and social concerns. Yet the left's re-evaluation of democracy took place within

---

1. Towards the end of military rule, in 1980, the MDB changed its name to PMDB (Partido do Movimento Democrático Brasileiro), in which guise it continues to be the largest political party in Brazil.

the framework of the liberal dominance of the anti-dictator-ship opposition, which also affected the PCB. As a result, democracy was incorporated into left debates at the expense of its class nature; capitalism as a general historical scenario disappeared altogether.

The key ideological text of the Brazilian left in this period was written in Italy by the exiled PCB intellectual Carlos Nelson Coutinho. 'Democracy as a Universal Value' was the most influential product of the PCB current that had been brought into direct contact with Eurocommunist ideas.[2] Coutinho took his cue from Enrico Berlinguer's interpretation of the fall of the Popular Unity coalition in Chile as a demonstration of the need to incorporate Christian Democrat forces, in order to prevent them from destabilizing a socialist government. The emphasis was placed on preserving democracy, rather than on the anti-capitalist dimensions of the struggle. Coutinho also sought to articulate the links between democracy and socialism, citing Lenin and Gramsci, but reading the latter in much the same way as had the PCI, resulting in similar contradictions.

Coutinho's text had broad repercussions on debates within the PCB, but its principal effect was on the eventual configuration taken by the PT. In a sense, he foretold the identity the party would adopt, notably when he affirmed that 'Brazilian *modernity* demands the creation of a secular, democratic, mass socialist party, capable of taking up what is valid in the heritage of Brazilian communism, but at the same time of incorporating the new socialist currents originating from different political and ideological horizons.'[3] Several others of Coutinho's statements were echoed by the PT. He was harshly critical of Jaruzelski's 'military coup' of 1981 which the PT also condemned, identifying itself with Lech Walesa's

---

2. Carlos Nelson Coutinho, *A democracia como valor universal*, Rio de Janeiro 1980.

3. Ibid., p. 13. Coutinho identified the PT as this force, and along with other PCB militants joined it in 1989. He was to leave it in the first year of the Lula government.

Solidarity movement.[4] Coutinho argued that Eurocommunism was the 'contemporary representative of the best traditions of the communist movement', in search of a 'third way' between 'the bureaucratic method of the Stalinists and neo-Stalinists' and the 'limited reformism of social democracy'.[5] The PT would seek the same equidistance, and later even proclaimed itself the 'first post-social-democratic party'.

In contrast to Coutinho, liberal opposition currents stressed the relationship between democracy and liberalism, rather than democracy and socialism. The principal exponent here was Cardoso, whose theory of authoritarianism became hegemonic during the transition from military dictatorship in the 1980s. In this version, democratization would consist of the 'de-concentration' of economic power from around the state, and of political power from around the executive. Brazil's first post-dictatorship civilian government in 1985, and new constitution of 1988, marked the onset of political de-concentration; its economic aspect would be set in motion by Cardoso himself, as president of Brazil from 1994–2002, with his neoliberal programme.

The triumphant advance of liberalism on the international plane in the 1980s was echoed in Brazil, above all in the strictly institutional nature of the passage from dictatorship to democracy; there were no significant social or economic reforms. The PT opposed this conservative model of transition, calling for citizens' rights and social policies; but it did not put forward any alternative conception of democracy, or question the notion that 'democratization' was the answer to the country's problems. Moreover, it failed to attend to the fact that the fall of the dictatorship also brought with it the end of a specific model of capital accumulation, inaugurated by Vargas in 1930 – and with it, a particular form of the state. The dominant liberal view, emphasizing political and juridical processes, obscured the deeper socio-economic crisis subtending that historical

---

4. Lula's first international trip was to meet Lech Walesa, at the prompting of the then international secretary of the PT, Francisco Weffort.

5. Coutinho, *Democracia*, p. 114.

moment. The PT identified itself with democracy; although it did mention socialism, the latter was never precisely defined, except to announce a distance from the Soviet model. Indeed, the PT often emphasized 'democracy' over 'socialism' – thus not only altering the meaning of the latter, but also plunging headlong into the contradictions liberal democracy was now installing in Brazil. Strikingly absent from the PT's founding manifesto and documents from the 1980s was any mention of capitalism: an indispensable reference for rethinking socialism.

Symbolically, it was in 1989 that the PT began to emerge as a genuine alternative for national government, with Lula's near victory in that year's election – he obtained 44 per cent of the vote in the second round, to Collor de Mello's 50 per cent.

The PT platform had two main axes: social justice and ethics in politics. The first, which had characterized the party since its creation, sought to add a social dimension to the process of democratization. The second was a response to the political scandals which marked the Sarney government, anticipating those that would lead to the impeachment of Collor. Yet this platform contained no specific proposals on the economy, the fiscal crisis facing the state or the political shape of the new democracy. These gaps show how little the left had understood the decline of the economic and state models prevalent from 1930 to 1980, or the rapid imposition of the neoliberal model in other parts of Latin America (Mexico, Argentina, Chile, Venezuela, Bolivia and Uruguay). It hoped that democratization would solve the country's problems through social policies and transparent politics. The references to socialism had no link with the PT's concrete analyses or proposals: these were rather an amalgam of democratization in the social sphere and moralization of the political one.

What determined the outcome of this battle was not Collor's narrow victory in 1989, but his ability to impose a new agenda, and the inability of the left to realize the depth of the crisis – a crisis of hegemony – that it was now facing. Collor pointed the way to a new hegemonic model based on two main principles: the critique of the public sector – accusing all public employees of being 'maharajas' and the state of being the villain of the Brazilian crisis because of its reckless spending – and that of the 'old bangers', a reference to the supposed technological backwardness of our industry, allegedly benefiting from excessive protectionism and blocking our access to 'modernity'. The roll-back of the state and opening up of the economy flowed automatically from these two principles. Privatizations, imports, cuts in public sector jobs and a violent seizure of resources through the freezing of bank deposits were the main planks of the new economic programme.

The left, for its part, hadn't grasped how things had changed internationally on the political and ideological terrain, now based on neoliberalism, and therefore failed to see that the conditions no longer existed for the old developmentalist model and the regulatory state. What was needed was to respond to the new challenges, as neoliberalism had already done in its own way. The left had to come up with alternatives to deal with the state's fiscal crisis, with the decline of the liberal political model and the mode of accumulation, which had gone into crisis as a result of the mushrooming foreign debt.

The 1994 elections were a turning point in the balance of forces in Brazil. Collor's victory in 1989 had *begun* the development of a neoliberal consensus, but the protests had continued and Collor's impeachment interrupted the first coherent attempt to implant a neoliberal model in Brazil. In 1994, Lula's lead through most of the campaign, then his decisive defeat by Fernando Henrique Cardoso, would have decisive consequences for the country, for the PT and for the Brazilian left.

The neoliberal consensus was consolidated right across the country, based on a series of rapid changes pushed through by the new government: a violent opening up of the economy, intensified privatization of state enterprises, withdrawal of the state from economic activity and roll-back of its social functions, deregulation, promotion of the market as the central axis of all economic activity, criminalization of social movements, disparagement of public-sector workers and introduction of a more flexible labour market. As far as he could, Fernando Henrique kept his promise to 'turn the page of *getulismo*[6] in Brazil', that is the national, regulatory, social state. At the same time the PT began, slowly to start with, a process of ideological adaptation that would eventually lead to the profile adopted by the Lula government eight years later.

Up until then, the PT had regarded the public deficit and its consequences – including inflation – as a secondary question. The turn in favour of Cardoso had an impact on the PT as well. The first significant aspect of this change – of particular symbolic importance – could be seen in the party's position on the foreign debt. From its initial stance in favour of not paying the debt, the policy shifted towards a suspension of payments with an audit, and ended up with the vow to respect all its commitments.

At the same time, the PT assimilated the consensus introduced by the previous government around the priority of combating inflation. Renewed inflation seemed a real risk, and Lula's image had always been linked to situations of risk that caused anxiety among broad sections of the middle class. The new concern with inflation, a leitmotiv of neoliberal hegemony, was therefore one of the most obvious pillars of the PT's ideological transformation.

These shifts went hand in hand with significant changes in the PT's social base. At a party congress held in Pernambuco state in December 2000, a poll revealed the changes in the make-up of delegates: more than 70 per cent of them had no history of grass-roots activism, but came from other kinds of backgrounds – party and union full-timers, parliamentary advisers, state enterprises, local governments, and so on. What's more, the average age had increased significantly and reflected a social base very different from that which had founded the party and made up its membership throughout, at least, the 1980s.

---

6. The nationalist, populist legacy of Getúlio Vargas. (*Translator's note*)

In addition to these changes, there was the overwhelming *ideological* hegemony of the new model: consumerism, the centrality of the market, the glorification of business and businessmen, shopping malls, TV advertising, etc – all of this under the benevolent eye of the mass-media monopolies. Individualism was held up over all forms of collective action; social movements were repressed and criminalized, especially the most combative ones, like the MST; the trade unions were put on the defensive; the world of labour vanished from the national debate. The link between political activity and mass mobilizations, a vital element of the left's strength in the 1980s, fell to a new low. The neoliberal offensive weakened the social movements, both socially and politically, while the PT was increasingly integrated into institutional politics. Both reflected a change in the balance of forces; the initiative had now passed to the right, with its political platform refurbished and fresh forces behind it.

When Lula stood for president in 1998, these ideological changes in the PT were already visible. Cardoso had pushed through an amendment to the constitution in order to be able to stand for re-election, and was the clear favourite to win. The PT displayed a marked lack of clarity in relation to the electoral success of the Real Plan.[7] The economy was on the verge of another crash, as became clear with the crisis of January 1999. Yet Lula, fearful of being associated with an image of crisis and catastrophe, decided not to touch on that subject. He was defeated in the first round, obtaining 32 per cent of the vote to Cardoso's 53, after a campaign in which he put forward no alternatives to the neoliberal model. Lula seemed resigned to the new consensus.

---

7. The *Plano Real*, first introduced by Fernando Henrique Cardoso when he was economy minister, became the centrepiece of his presidency. It was a markedly neoliberal package, which won a significant measure of public support in so far as it succeeded in curbing Brazil's hyper-inflation crisis of the early 1990s. (*Translator's note*)

THE ROAD TO THE PLANALTO

After the 1998 defeat, Lula and his advisers moved to set up the Institute of Citizenship, a think tank outside PT structures. It enabled Lula to become increasingly independent of the PT – expressing, in organizational terms, the far greater public projection he enjoyed compared to the party. The Institute organized seminars attended by economists and specialists in other areas – social policy, environment and political reform, among others – in order to formulate Lula's campaign programme for 2002. The final version, which would be ratified by the PT, stressed what were to be the two key themes of the campaign: the 'priority of the social', and the resumption of development, as a precondition for the former. An opposition was established between productive and speculative capital – without distinguishing between foreign and national capital, large and small firms, industrial or other enterprises. Reviving the economy was to be the major objective, presaging a slow, gradual exit from the neoliberal model. Campaign publicity emphasized 'change' and the 'priority of the social'. There were no concrete indications of what was meant by this priority, but the forms it would take once the PT was in government could already be discerned: the 'Zero Hunger' campaign echoed Lula's repeated statements in 2002, and in earlier electoral contests, that his goal was for 'all Brazilians to eat three times a day'. Mention was also made of the need to maintain monetary stability, a programme which by implication already included many of the Lula government's subsequent proposals – such as the reform of social security.

Cardoso's campaign slogan in 1998 had been 'He who puts an end to inflation puts an end to unemployment'. By 2002 his record on both fronts was clear. The economy had not recovered from the crisis of 1999, and monetary stability had not brought renewed development, still less any extension of social policies. Unlike in 1998, Lula now appeared a strong candidate, although opinions polls suggested voters wanted a president who would combine monetary stability with social policies – criteria effectively in line with the Buenos Aires Consensus and, among the main candidates, matched most closely by Ciro Gomes.

Two factors helped to determine the outcome of the election. The first was the candidacy of Ciro Gomes, the other the strong speculative attack on the *real* carried out by finance capital in the summer of 2002, a few months before the vote. At the start of the campaign both Lula and Gomes found themselves behind in the polls, led at that stage by Roseana Sarney, daughter of ex-president José Sarney. The government candidate José Serra, then health minister, came a distant fourth, before he orchestrated a string of denunciations that effectively removed Sarney from the race. But Serra still faced elimination in the first round, and so he began a new round of denunciations, this time aimed at Gomes. The latter's standing in the polls dwindled, but Serra – who was, as Cardoso's man, vulnerable to the same criticisms Gomes had made of the incumbent – failed to close the gap on Lula who, in turn, remained unable to break through the PT's historic ceiling of slightly over 30 per cent of the vote. The attack on the *real* was a show of force on the part of finance capital, as if to underline both its potential stabilizing role and its ability to sabotage any new government to which it objected. The message was that the return of capital to the country would depend on the result. The 'Brazil risk' began to be known as the 'Lula risk', implying that in the event of a PT victory, monetary destabilization and uncontrolled capital flight would ensue – resulting in a sharp drop in the value of the *real* in July 2002.

But in June 2002 Lula, condemning the speculative attack, had released a document entitled 'Letter to the Brazilians', in which he pledged that, as president, he would keep to all the previous government's financial commitments. There would be no renegotiation of the external debt, nor any regulation of the movement of finance capital. The PT had gradually softened its position on external debt over the past decade; the shift from suspension of payments to renegotiation marked its first steps on the path to becoming a potential party of government, culminating in Lula's 2002 commitment to pay the debt in full. Monetary stability, too, had steadily increased in importance as a strategic objective after the 1994 election defeat; on Lula's accession it became a general filter for all government activity. But it was above all the 'Letter' that altered the Lula campaign's relationship with finance capital and, in the process, changed its social character and relation to the neoliberal model. The physiognomy of the future Lula government was beginning to take shape.

The transformation was apparent even during Lula's electoral campaign, when decision-making was transferred to the marketing chief Duda Mendonça, who had previously run the campaigns of the prominent right-winger Paulo Maluf, and to Antonio Palocci, former PT governor of Ribeirão Preto in São Paulo state, one of Brazil's richest cities, and the man behind Lula's economic programme and the 'Letter to the Brazilians'. Mendonça devised the slogan 'Lulinha, Peace and Love' in an attempt to soften his candidate's pugilistic image, forged in union organizing and polemical critique of the policies and corruption of the political elite. (In the 1990s, Lula had said that there were 300 'pickaxes' in Congress – slang for shamelessly immoral characters.) The slogan and 'Letter' proved a winning combination – the former deployed so often as to virtually become the content of a campaign which was increasingly that of Lula, and not of the PT. In addition, Lula had picked the textile magnate José Alencar as his running mate, and had the support of the conservative Partido Trabalhista Brasileiro. Street-level activism and public rallies played a far less prominent role than in previous elections, and the level of PT mobilization further diminished after 2002. This was the basis on which Lula won the presidency in the second round of the election, with 61 per cent of the vote to Serra's 39 per cent.

The Lula government introduced a difficult and contradictory cohabitation between, on the one hand, the hegemony of finance capital – expressed in the de facto autonomy of the Central Bank and the continuity of the previous government's

financial policy, giving priority to fiscal adjustment and monetary stability over social spending – and, on the other hand,
redistributive social policies and an independent foreign policy.
In this framework, where it was the economic and financial
team that called the shots, social policies could not be universal in character, as they would have been if the government's
priorities had been creating jobs, expanding the domestic consumer market and securing social rights for everyone. That
would have meant systematically increasing wages, extending
land reform and improving access to sanitation, health care,
education and culture, as well as supporting food security
and small-scale family agriculture, among other clear social
measures.

Instead, social policy followed criteria of targeted social
assistance, combining various mechanisms like the Family
Allowance (*Bolsa Familia*), granted in exchange for keeping
children in school, micro-credit programmes, systematic
increases in the minimum wage, boosts to formal employment,
price controls on food and electrification in the countryside. Through these mechanisms, some of the PT's original
objectives *were* attained, at least in part: income redistribution, rise in formal employment, expansion of the domestic
mass consumer market, and so on. The result was a general
improvement in the standard of living of the poorest sections
of society, especially in the Northeast and in the slums of the
big metropolitan centres; for the first time, inequality in the
country began to diminish.[8]

Initially it was the dictatorship of fiscal discipline, represented by the presence of Antonio Palocci as finance minister
for the first three years of his first term in office, that defined
Lula's government. Any kind of mobilization was discouraged;
the policy did not generate a new cycle of economic growth,
nor did it allow the government to prioritize social policy.

---

8. To dismiss this as 'assistentialist' is reductionist and misses the significance of transforming the lives of 50 million of the poorest people in Brazil, by
giving them access for the first time to goods and forms of consumption that are
essential for a dignified life.

Exorbitant interest rates and Palocci's overweening power to control the flow of resources to all areas of government acted like a tourniquet, blocking action in key areas. Innovation by the new government was limited to foreign policy (Brazil played a leading part in finally eliminating the proposal for a Free Trade Area of the Americas (FTAA), thereby opening the way to new forms of regional integration), and cultural policy, thanks to the considerable creativity of Culture Minister Gilberto Gil.[9]

The elements of continuity with the Cardoso government were clear: on financial policy, with the central objective as monetary stability, reflected in high interest rates; on the independence of the Central Bank; on ensuring a primary fiscal surplus; on the dominant role of exports, especially primary commodities like genetically modified soya. The elements of difference – which coincide with the government's positive points – had to do mostly with foreign and social policy, but also with the significant increase in formal employment, the rebuilding of the state apparatus and its ability to promote development, something that had been eliminated by the previous government but was now firmly back on the national agenda. There was a move from total alignment behind US foreign policy – which could have led to Brazil becoming the main sponsor for the FTAA (ALCA in its Spanish acronym) – to a position that favoured regional integration in Latin America and across the South. While Brazil, jointly with the United States, presided over the FTAA negotiations, it decided to block its implementation and opted for Mercosur as an alternative to free-trade treaties.

---

9. Gilberto Gil is a Brazilian singer-songwriter, one of the best-known figures of the MPB (Brazilian Popular Music) movement that emerged in the late 1960s, who became minister of culture in President Lula's first administration. (*Translator's note*)

MEASURING THE ENIGMA

The result of these policies is a hybrid that is difficult to characterize. As Lula himself said when he was re-elected: 'Never have the rich made so much money, nor the poor improved so much their standard of living'. Any one-sided analysis leads to serious mistakes. So much so that it is easier to say what the Lula government is not, than what it really is.

There are those who describe it as 'a tropical version of Blairism', that is, of the European 'third way'. An attempt was made to copy this in Latin America with the so-called Buenos Aires consensus, coordinated by Jorge Castañeda and Roberto Mangabeira Unger, with the participation of politicians like Ciro Gomes and various PT leaders.[10] Their aim was to 'humanize neoliberalism and globalization'. The central principles of privatizations allegedly necessary to pay off public debts – fiscal adjustment and monetary stability – were incorporated into what became known as 'social-liberalism', a 'third way' between Reagan and Thatcher's market fundamentalism – represented in Latin America by Pinochet, but also by Menem and Cardoso, among others – and an approach where the state would play a strategic part. It showed clearly how monetary stability had become a part of the new regional consensus.

From the 'Letter to the Brazilians' to the formation of the government and the announcement of its two chief priorities, everything confirmed the new course being charted by the PT. A big international banker, ex-Bank of Boston general manager Henrique Meirelles, was nominated as governor of the Central Bank, while tax reform and pension reform were to be key objectives (both of them what the World Bank called 'second-generation reforms'). The economic model was

---

10. Jorge Castañeda is a former left-wing Mexican intellectual and biographer of Che Guevara who moved to the right in the 1990s and served as foreign minister from 2000–2003 under President Vicente Fox. Roberto Mangabeira Unger is a well-known Brazilian social theorist, who taught Barack Obama at Harvard Law School and served as a minister during Lula's second term. (*Translator's note*)

retained, although somewhat ambiguously it was described as a 'cursed legacy', responsible for the precarious state of the economy. According to the then all-powerful minister Palocci, using the language of a doctor dressed up as an economist, 'you don't change the treatment in the middle of the illness'. The model was preserved, and conservative attitudes vindicated. In January 2003, at the first meeting of the Monetary Policy Committee (COPOM), the Central Bank raised the already very high interest rate from 25 per cent to 25.5 per cent against Lula's stated wish, showing its independence from the government and signalling to big business the continuity with the previous orientation. And the new president – who during his electoral campaign had repeatedly promised to take his ministers on a journey to get to know the real Brazil and the cruel social impact of high interest rates – now gave in to the dynamic he had inherited, giving it his blessing during his very first month in office.

Lula's message stressed these two reforms ostensibly as a way of reassuring markets and investors, and thereby creating the conditions to return to growth and prioritize social needs. After all, that was why he had been elected: to ensure that all Brazilians could eat three meals a day – something Lula regarded as 'a revolution'.

This continuation of the previous model meant, in fact, that the economy was unable to return to growth; the consequence was the negligible impact of social policies, a minuscule increase in the minimum wage, the slow pace of land reform, a growing estrangement between social movements and the government and a disheartening message overall, suggesting that this administration would continue to play by neoliberal rules and fail to keep the social promises that Lula had made.

It was in this context that the government suffered a series of blows that threatened its stability and even its existence, with consequences that neither friend nor foe had anticipated. A campaign of aggressive attacks on the government, accusing it of buying political allies, undermined the central core of the administration, forcing Lula to get rid of most of his closest aides, including, as the crisis unfolded, Antonio Palocci himself.

The reshuffle that the president was forced to make gave a new shape to the government. Two main changes set the tone for this new line-up, beginning three and a half years into the government's first mandate. The appointment of the future president, Dilma Rousseff, as chief of staff, charged with co-coordinating the government's economic and social programmes, as well as the replacement of Palocci with Guido Mantega, a developmentalist who would not continue the previous orientation of the Finance Ministry, were responsible for changes that, without any major ruptures, would set a new course. It was because of these that Lula won re-election in 2006, and by the end of his second term in office enjoyed 87 per cent popular support.

The government did not change the central pillars of its economic policy, like the fiscal surplus, the de facto independence of the Central Bank and the key part played by agribusiness exports, especially soya and other GM crops. However, supported by a favourable international situation, it was able to free up resources for social policies and re-balance its actions. Especially with the Accelerated Growth Programme (PAC), a discrepancy became apparent – even a contradiction – between conservative financial policy and developmentalist economic policy. The return of economic growth was at odds with analyses which suggested that neither growth nor redistributive social policies would be possible without a break from the neoliberal model. This view failed to grasp the changes in the government, or to make a distinction between financial and economic policies. It didn't recognize that the latter had enabled a huge extension of social policies, which were no longer targeted – as they had been in the first, now abandoned, version of the Zero Hunger Programme – but had taken on a mass character.

This new expansive cycle combined exports, diversification of the external market and an extension of the domestic market, this time with a decisive part being played by mass

popular consumption, to promote a return to growth. At the
same time the social policies mentioned above produced, for
the first time in Brazil's history, a reversal of income distribution trends in favour of the poor: the so-called D and E classes
ceased to be the majority of the population, with this position
now being occupied by class C, which in 2007 accounted for
46 per cent of the population.[11] Formal employment, although
mostly unskilled or semi-skilled, grew continuously, reversing
one of the worst, if not *the* worst effect of neoliberalism on the
mass of the population.

However, another major negative effect of neoliberalism
has not been contained: the financialization of the economy.
The highest real interest rates in the world, total liquidity with
almost no taxation, the effective autonomy of the Central
Bank and the insistence on securing a primary surplus, are all
expressions of this. The incentives for agribusiness exports, as
we have pointed out, conflict with land reform, family agriculture and food security; they are part of an alliance between
the government and big capital, led by finance capital, in the
multi-class bloc currently in power.

In 2010, Lula's chosen candidate to succeed him, the same
Dilma Rousseff who had co-ordinated government policy for
five successful years, based her presidential campaign on the
pledge to continue that success. The opposition fielded the man
Lula had beaten in 2002, José Serra. He swung from posing as
the best choice to prolong Lula's legacy, at the beginning of the
campaign, to adopting an openly right-wing stance as soon as
Rousseff overtook him in the polls.

Since any comparison between the Cardoso and Lula governments clearly favoured the latter and his candidate, the
opposition sought to shift the debate onto conservative themes
where religious forces – mainly Evangelical but also Catholic – wielded considerable influence, including the question
of abortion. This manoeuvre enabled them to take the election to a second round and, even though she won, to reduce

11. Classes D and E together accounted for 39 per cent (*Pesquisa Observador
2008*, March 2008).

Rousseff's vote to a third less than Lula's own approval rating at the time.

CONCLUSIONS

It can be said that the glass is half full, or that it is half empty. The Lula government can be seen as a good manager of neoliberalism, one which both continued the model and customized it with social policies and a revalidation of the state, which had been so weakened by the more orthodox neoliberalism of Fernando Henrique Cardoso. But it can also be seen as a government with an independent foreign policy, which scuppered the FTAA and promoted regional integration instead, forming alliances with the governments of Hugo Chávez, Rafael Correa, Evo Morales and others, including Cuba. It is also the government that halted the erosion of the state, strengthened the public health and education systems, and creatively expanded cultural policy. Above all, it is the government that has done most to improve the living standards of the masses, especially the poorest sectors, in the most unequal country in Latin America, itself the most unequal region in the world.

The first of these possible interpretations led far-left tendencies to regard the Lula government as the main enemy. Allying themselves with the traditional right, including with its main stronghold in the private media, these groups ignored the positive aspects of the record. They failed in their attempt to build a force to the left of the PT, precisely because they refused any kind of alliance with this party and insisted instead on direct confrontation; this made for still greater confusion with the right, which remained staunchly opposed to the Lula government. As a result, the polarization of national politics is clearly between the government and the right-wing opposition, leaving the latter as the only alternative to Lula, with no possibilities open to the left, now completely neutralized.

Looking at the Lula government in terms of its contradictions, on the other hand, makes it possible to distinguish its positive elements, and fight to strengthen these, as against its conservative elements. It also makes it possible to struggle for an anti-neoliberal platform, in order to prompt Lula's successor to advance in this direction. At the same time it allows us to work for the international alliances that favour governments like those of Bolivia, Venezuela, Ecuador and Cuba, and positions the left to take on its other great task, which is to help organize the vast numbers of the poor who support Lula, and promote their economic and social rights.

In any balance sheet of pros and cons, other aspects must be taken into account. On the negative side, there is the lack of stimulus for, even repression of community radios; the slow demarcation of indigenous lands, as well as of land reform; the failure to open the archives of the dictatorship, and so on. On the positive side, there are educational and cultural policies and the creation of a public TV, among others. The lists could go on, but they wouldn't produce any clear result for or against. Political analysis is qualitative, basing itself on general strategic criteria.

In this case, the criteria that we identify as crucial for Latin America apply to Brazil as well: priority for regional integration as against free trade treaties, and the promotion of economic and social rights for the poorest sectors, all the more so in a country with such high levels of inequality. According to these criteria which characterize the Latin American governments, it is the progressive character of the Lula government that predominates: it has contributed to a multi-polar world and prioritized regional integration and South–South alliances; what's more, it has played an important role in the Group of 20 and other similar initiatives.

But this characterization is not a matter of foreign policy alone. The rejection of the FTAA and the priority given to alliances with Latin America and the South has a much greater significance: it also implies insisting on a bigger role for the state in the economy, broadening the domestic, mass consumer market, increasing formal employment and strengthening public health and education.

We cannot lose sight, therefore, of the fact that this was a hybrid, contradictory government, in which on the one hand finance capital played an essential role, and, on the other, there was an increasing development of redistributive social policies, as well as state regulation and the reduction of informal labour relations.

After a defensive period for the left that lasted right through the 1990s, the Lula government sent ambiguous signals: it didn't implement the PT's historic programme, it didn't base its actions on the ideas of the World Social Forum, carry out the land reform demanded by the MST or incorporate the participatory budget into its platform. Judged by the traditional criteria of the Brazilian left, it seemed an alien phenomenon. Nonetheless, judged against the background of the Cardoso government and the balance of forces in the period of neoliberal and North American imperial hegemony, the differences are sufficient to characterize it as a distinct kind of government. The crucial difference is that, in 1989, a government of the left would have encountered a national and international balance of forces quite unlike that with which the Lula government had to deal at the beginning of the new century.

The neoliberal era – and the situation which this introduced in Latin America and Brazil, with the governments of Collor and Fernando Henrique Cardoso – imposed a new political framework, whose dynamics require analysis. The entire political scene shifted towards the centre and the right, not just in relation to people's opinions, but in relation to the very topics of concern. A number of questions came to the fore, born of a conservative agenda and promoted by the right-wing media, which the left seemed unable either to answer with convincing alternatives, or to displace from the spotlight.

Issues like the struggle against inflation, allegedly excessive taxation, law and order, or the identification of press freedom with private media and of democracy with liberal democracy, all came to occupy the centre of the political and ideological stage and to define what was supposed to be public opinion. The campaigns to criminalize land occupations painted a violent picture of the landless movement, as if they were the ones responsible for violence in the countryside. The critique of the state – on grounds of cost, taxes, bureaucracy, regulations, the inefficiency of public services, corruption and favouritism – projected an utterly negative image of all things public.

These regressive ideological changes went hand in hand with a mounting moderation on the part of political parties as they redefined their identities, and a weakening of the social movements' capacity to mobilize. At the same time, globalization encouraged ever more open economies, with more weight for finance capital and increasingly international companies. This was an evident reality in countries like Brazil, Mexico, Argentina, Chile, Peru and Colombia. There the social foundations for a national, popular bloc, of the kind that had existed in the past, simply vanished. Big capital in its various forms became more international, either in its composition or in the way it was integrated into vast, international circuits of realization. Combined with the retreat in the organization of social movements and in social awareness, this resulted in a profoundly detrimental change for the struggles of the left. In such circumstances, the fight against neoliberalism was the best starting point for the left to regain the initiative and resume its historic struggle against capitalism and for socialism.

That is why, in our countries, to work against the privatization of public companies, the enfeeblement of the state, and the operations of an increasingly precarious labour market, while fortifying the domestic consumer market, the ability of the state to regulate and carry out social policies, and foreign policies that emphasize regional integration, are contributions that cannot be underestimated for the rebuilding of the left. The alternative today is a sterile and misguided frontal opposition to governments like those of Lula, the Kirchners, Tabaré Vázquez and Fernando Lugo, one that equates them with their predecessors without recognizing the differences. Such analyses are one-sided, fail to recognize the contradictory character of these governments and do not give any credit to their positive aspects.

Two strategies are possible in the face of contradictory and hybrid governments like these. One is all-out opposition, as we have said. The consequences of this are isolation and a retreat into doctrinaire and ultra-left positions, with no capacity whatever to gather support and develop alternative projects and blocs. This is a strategy based on the idea that the government, whether of Lula, Kirchner or Tabaré Vázquez, is the main enemy to be defeated; and since these governments supposedly represent the new right, it is even justified to ally against them with the traditional right.

The second strategy involves an alliance with the progressive sectors of these governments, with the aim of strengthening these sectors and concentrating the attack on the hegemony of finance capital, the agreements with agribusiness, the autonomy of the Central Bank and other negative aspects.

These are the two available options. Only one of them makes it possible to link up with the other experiences in Latin America, those of the Venezuelans, Bolivians, Ecuadoreans and Cubans – and to begin to build support for the left in Brazil as well.

4

Orphans of Strategy?

Although a continent of revolutions and counter-revolutions, Latin America lacks the strategic thinking it needs to orient its rich variety of political experiences, which is adequate to the challenges it faces. In spite of considerable analytical skills, important processes of change and a number of emblematic revolutionary leaders, the continent has not yet produced the theory of its own practice.

The three historic strategies of the left have had dynamic forces in their leadership – Socialist and Communist parties, nationalist movements and guerrilla groups – and have steered experiences of profound political significance such as the Cuban Revolution, the government of Salvador Allende, the Sandinista victory, the post-neoliberal governments in Venezuela, Bolivia and Ecuador, the building of local power, as in Chiapas, and the experiments with participatory budgets, of which the most important were developed in the city of Porto Alegre. Nonetheless, there is no overall, strategic vision that could combine assessments of these different approaches and a number of other reflections into a set of new proposals.

The fact that these three strategies were developed by distinct political forces means there has been no shared process of common activity, reflection and synthesis. While they still had a real presence, the communist parties encouraged theoretical reflection on their own experiences. During its short lifespan, the OLAS (Latin American Solidarity Organization) did the same for the processes of armed struggle. The nationalist movements, for their part, never had enough contact with each other to produce anything similar. Today's processes have allowed little room for theory, or for critically examining the new realities.

The strategies adopted in Latin America suffered badly, above all in the early days, from the left's international links, especially with the communist parties, but also with the social democrats. The 'class against class' line introduced in the second half of the 1920s was a direct import from the Soviet Union, where it reflected the isolation from Western European governments, and was not based on concrete conditions in Latin America. As a result, it made it difficult to understand the particular political forms taken by the response to the crisis of 1929 – of which the government of Getúlio Vargas in Brazil was just one expression, alongside the fleeting socialist government in Chile, that lasted just twelve days, and similar phenomena in Cuba.

The revolts led by Farabundo Martí in El Salvador and Augusto Sandino in Nicaragua were born of the specific circumstances of resistance to North American occupation and were direct expressions of anti-imperialist nationalism. The processes of industrialization in Argentina, Brazil and Mexico came in response to the 1929 crisis. There was not, at least to begin with, any developed strategy behind them. The Economic Commission for Latin America and the Caribbean (CEPAL)[1]

---

1. CEPAL was set up in 1948 as the body of the United Nations responsible for encouraging economic and social development in the region, with its headquarters in Santiago, Chile. Under its first Executive Secretary, the Argentinean economist Raúl Prebisch, from 1950 to 1963, it became an influential promoter of structuralist economic analyses and developmentalist policies. (*Translator's note*)

was merely describing an existing state of affairs when, at the beginning of the postwar period, it began to develop its theory of import-substitution industrialization, which in any case was a purely economic strategy. Nor did the 1952 Bolivian Revolution elaborate a strategy of its own; rather it put into practice a number of existing demands, like universal suffrage, land reform and the nationalization of the mines.

Thus neither nationalism nor traditional reformism based their action on strategies; they simply responded to economic, political and social demands. When the Communist International adopted its position on anti-fascist fronts in 1935, application of the new policy clashed with the concrete circumstances in Latin American countries. If the 'class against class' line corresponded to conditions inside the USSR, the new orientation was a response to the growth of fascism in Europe. Neither took account of the situation in Latin America, which was just thrown in alongside the colonial periphery in general, with no particular identity of its own.

This failure had various consequences. For example, the Brazilian movement led by Luis Carlos Prestes, in 1935, found itself caught between these two contradictory, imported political lines.[2] On the one hand, they organized an uprising based on the 'lieutenants', in keeping with the more confrontational 'class against class' orientation; on the other, they advocated not a workers' and peasants' government, but a national liberation front, in accordance with the new, broader orientation of the Communist International. In other words, the form of struggle corresponded to the earlier, radical line, while the objective reflected the more moderate one of a democratic front. The result was that the movement isolated itself from the nationalist, popular 'Revolution of 30', led by Getúlio Vargas.

The Popular Front in Chile imported the 'anti-fascist' slogan, even though fascism had barely reached the continent.

---

2. Luis Carlos Prestes was a junior officer in the Brazilian military who led a revolt and a 'long march' in the 1920s, spent time in the Soviet Union, became a leader of the Brazilian Communist Party and led a failed uprising by the National Liberation Alliance (ALN) in 1935. (*Translator's note*)

This was a mechanical transfer of the analysis of European fascism to Latin America, with all the mistakes that flowed from that. In Europe, fascism had taken a stance that was nationalist and anti-liberal, but in no sense anti-imperialist. European nationalism was characterized by chauvinism, by the supposed superiority of one national state over others and by opposition to liberalism, including liberal democracy. This liberal ideology had been taken up by the rising bourgeoisie as a means of releasing the free circulation of capital from its feudal fetters.

In Latin America too, nationalism was both politically and economically anti-liberal; but it also took an anti-imperialist stance, because of its position on the periphery – in our case in relation to the United States – which put it on the side of the left. However, the mechanical copying of European schemas of fascism and anti-fascism led some communist parties (for example in Brazil and Argentina), on occasions, to characterize Juan Perón and Getúlio Vargas as reproductions of fascism in Latin America, and therefore identified them as mortal enemies to be fought. The Argentinean Communist Party, for example, in the 1945 elections, in opposition to Perón, allied itself not only with the liberal candidate, of the Radical Party, but with the Church and the US Embassy, on the grounds that any alliance was justified against the main enemy, which was fascism.

The main confusion has to do not just with nationalism, but also with liberalism, which in Europe was the ideology of the bourgeoisie in its ascendancy, but which in Latin America was taken up, along with free trade, by the oligarchies that controlled primary commodity exports. Not only nationalism, but liberalism too has exactly the opposite significance here.

It was this that produced a separation between the social and the democratic, and the incorporation of social questions into the nationalist agenda, at the expense of democratic ones. Liberalism always sought to lay claim to the theme of democracy, and to accuse nationalist governments of being authoritarian, totalitarian and dictatorial. These, in turn, accused the

liberals of governing for the rich and of lacking social awareness, while claiming themselves to defend the impoverished
mass of the population.

Only the concrete analyses of concrete situations, like
those developed by, among others, the Peruvian José Carlos
Mariátegui, the Cuban Julio Antonio Mella, the Chilean Luis
Emilio Recabarren and the Brazilian Caio Prado Jr.[3] – all of
them independent analyses which were largely ignored by the
communist parties of which all these were members – would
have made it possible to take on board the specific historical
conditions of each country and the region as a whole. But it
was the perspectives of the Communist International that held
sway, and made it more difficult for the communist parties to
sink roots in these countries.

When nationalism *was* taken up by the left, it was as a subordinate force in alliances with popular leaders representing
multi-class blocs. This long period was never theorized by the
left, and the alliances and theories put forward by the popular
fronts did not understand this new phenomenon, where anti-
imperialism took the place of anti-fascism, with very different
characteristics.

There was a dispute over how to interpret the Bolivian
Revolution of 1952, because it contained both nationalist elements, like the nationalization of the tin mines, and popular
ones, like land reform. But the active role of workers' militias,
taking the place of the army, the existence of a worker–peasant
alliance and the inclusion of anti-capitalist demands, enabled
other interpretations of what was emerging from this multi-
class movement, ranging from a classic nationalism of an
anti-oligarchic bent, to different versions of anti-capitalism.

The Cuban Revolution could count on two kinds of theoretical support: the programmatic one of Fidel in *History Will
Absolve Me*, and that of Che in *Guerrilla Warfare*, on the
strategy for building a political-military force and struggling

3. The first three were early leaders and theoreticians of the communist
movement in Peru, Cuba and Chile respectively. Caio Prado Jr. was a Brazilian
Communist intellectual active in the 1930s and '40s. *(Translator's note)*

for power. The text that Fidel wrote as his defence in the trial of those who attacked the Moncada Barracks, in 1952, is an extraordinary exercise in developing a political programme on the basis of the concrete conditions of Cuban society at the time. Che's analysis describes in concrete detail how the guerrilla war combined political and military struggle, from the initial guerrilla nucleus to large detachments of the rebel army; how it resisted the offensive of the regular army, and how it launched the final offensive that led to victory.

However, either because they hadn't thought about it, or because they wanted to maintain an element of surprise – which could be important for victory – there was never any public attempt to explain the character of the movement, defining whether it was merely nationalist, or embryonically anti-capitalist. It was in the light of unfolding events that the Cuban Revolution developed its strategy for a rapid transition from the democratic and national phase to the anti-imperialist and anti-capitalist phase, as the dynamic between revolution and counter-revolution dictated. This development was much less discussed than the forms of struggle, especially guerrilla warfare, which occasioned *the* major debate in Latin America after the Cuban victory. Armed struggle or peaceful road? Guerrilla war or people's war? Urban guerrillas or rural guerrillas? The link between national or anti-imperialist questions and anti-capitalist or socialist ones was far less discussed and theorized.

The various guerrilla struggles and the Popular Unity government in Chile prolonged this central debate. Nationalist military governments, especially that of Velasco Alvarado in Peru, but also, fleetingly, those in Ecuador and Honduras, raised the question of nationalism again, but their military character did not encourage the left at the time to analyse their dynamics or to consider them as strategic alternatives.

The Nicaraguan revolution incorporated earlier strategies for taking power and elaborated a rather vague governmental platform which took account of a series of new factors. The most important of these were the arrival of large numbers of Christians and women into the revolutionary ranks, and a more flexible foreign policy. Obstacles were dealt with in an empirical way – most notably, the military siege mounted by the United States. Yet the platform produced little or no theory to explain what was being done.

As with Popular Unity, the Sandinista experience generated a vast bibliography. But this hardly led to a clear strategic balance sheet, capable of leaving lessons for the left as a whole. The debate about Chile became a part of the international discussions on the left, and thus lost its Chilean or Latin American specificity. The debates about Nicaragua, on the other hand, raised important issues, for example of ethics. But they did not produce a strategic assessment of the eleven years of Sandinista government.

Just when the left was at its weakest around the world, the Brazilian left appeared as an exception; it seemed to be moving against the general current, especially in comparison with the radically regressive turn-about in the international balance of forces. Here Lula projected himself as a political alternative from the very first time he stood for president, in 1989. By reaching the second round he helped the left, for the first time, to look like a viable governmental alternative in Brazil – in the same year as the fall of the Berlin Wall and the end of the socialist camp, with strong signs that the Soviet Union was about to fall apart and the United States about to win the Cold War, delivering the world to the uncontested, imperial hegemony of the United States.

At the same time, Carlos Menem and Carlos Andrés Pérez won in Argentina and Venezuela, thereby extending the neo-liberal experience to nationalist and social-democratic forces and indicating the spread of these policies to the whole of the continent. To this would be added the election of Fernando Collor de Mello, who in the end defeated Lula, and of the Concertación, an alliance between Christian Democracy and the Socialist Party, in Chile in 1990. In February of the same year came the electoral defeat of the Sandinistas in Nicaragua. Cuba had entered into its 'special period', during which it would confront, with considerable difficulty, the consequences of the end of the socialist camp, into which it had been structurally integrated.

Meanwhile a number of developments in Brazil pointed towards a new kind of left – post-Soviet according to some, post-social-democratic according to others. In addition to Lula and the PT, the 1980s had seen the foundation of the CUT, the first legally-recognized trade union congress in the country's history; the emergence of the MST, the country's strongest and most innovative social movement, and the beginnings of participatory budgets in local government, generally in municipalities governed by the PT. For all these reasons, the southern Brazilian city of Porto Alegre would later be chosen to host the World Social Forums.

All of this meant that great hopes were placed on the Brazilian left, and especially on the PT and Lula's leadership – hopes that a new phase was opening for a renovated left. Yet as the previous chapter's analysis suggests, these expectations were hardly justified by the real situation of the party and its leader, or the political and ideological characteristics these had developed over the years.

Some parts of the left, and some international currents, painted Lula as a class-struggle, workers' leader, linked to the traditions of workers' councils, as well as the leader of a new, Gramscian kind of left party, at once socialist and democratic. Lula was nothing of the sort. Nor was he a leader in the image of what the PT had become. Lula's origins were as a grass-roots, trade union leader in the period when trade unions were banned by the dictatorship, a leader who negotiated directly with the bosses, a great mass leader, but without ideology. He felt no connection with the left tradition, neither with its ideological currents nor with its historical experiences. He joined what we might call the social left, without necessarily having any political or ideological links to it. He sought to improve the conditions of either the working masses, the people or the country, according to the evolution of his own vocabulary over the course of his career. He is a negotiator at heart, averse to confrontation, and therefore with no radical bent for revolution.

One aspect of the hegemonic crisis in Latin America is the lack of any accompanying theorization. In general the post-neoliberal processes have advanced by trial and error, along the lines of least resistance in the neoliberal chain. The work of the Bolivian group, Comuna, is a notable exception. They have produced the richest collection of texts that the Latin American left has to draw on. It's a unique example, because they have been able to combine individual and academic works of great theoretical creativity by writers like Álvaro García Linera, Luis Tapia and Raúl Prada, among others, with direct political interventions – so much so that García Linera became vice-president of the Republic, and Raúl Prada was a leading member of the constituent assembly.

These processes have already gone beyond the initial phase, when – as we pointed out – they made progress relatively easily, until the right reorganized and regained its capacity for initiative. Since then it has become essential, for any further advance, that we develop theories that will allow us to understand the real historical situation that the region confronts, with its strengths and weaknesses, the real, concrete and global balance of forces, the challenges and possible solutions.

Ever since the neoliberal hegemony took hold, resistance to this model and the struggles of the social movements, including the World Social Forum, have shifted the focus of their thinking to the arena of denunciation and resistance, and neglected to reflect on political and strategic questions. In other words the emphasis has been on working in the area of so-called civil society, to the detriment of politics, the state and, with these, issues of strategy and the construction of alternative hegemonic projects and new political and social blocs. This theoretical stance has severely diminished the analytical capacity of the anti-neoliberal forces, which have virtually limited themselves to celebrating the voices of resistance and grassroots mobilizations, while ignoring the positions of parties and governments.

The new social movements had no updated, Latin American, strategic thinking to draw on – not even balance sheets of previous positive and negative experiences. What made the situation even more serious were the deep changes in the historic period, notably the shift from a bipolar to a unipolar world, under US imperial hegemony, and from a regulated model to a neoliberal one. These were changes on a world scale, with consequences for Latin America. One of these was the step backward in the way the countries of the region were inserted into the world economy, as a result of the neoliberal lifting of trade barriers and the debilitation of national states.

Theories like those of John Holloway and Toni Negri seemed to accommodate to the way things were; instead of putting forward strategic solutions, they made a virtue of their absence. Although they used different theoretical frameworks, both ended up supporting the congenital lack of strategy on the part of those who rejected the state and politics, and took refuge in a mythical 'civil society' and a reductionist 'autonomy of the social movements'. Such a renunciation of strategic thinking and propositions left the anti-neoliberal camp unprepared to meet the challenges presented by the hegemonic crisis, which became more acute as the dispute over hegemony came to the fore.

Post-neoliberalism brings new theoretical challenges. The new circumstances that social and political struggles face in the region mean a new kind of practice needs to be explained, and that requires strategic reflection and proposals which point towards new forms of power.

Several things make it difficult for the Latin American left today to theorize its practice. One of them is the way theoretical work is mainly concentrated in universities, where the change in period had a particular impact: through the ideological offensive of neoliberalism; because people get trapped in the universities' internal division of labour, especially through specialization; and due to the tendency to take refuge in merely critical positions, often quite doctrinaire ones, without pointing to any alternatives.

Meanwhile the real struggles to overcome neoliberalism have raised issues that are far removed from academic reflection. Issues like the indigenous peoples and pluri-national states, the nationalization of natural resources, regional integration, or the new nationalism and post-neoliberalism have little to do with the topics usually included in university courses or those favoured by research institutions. The latter have promoted a fragmented approach, giving no credit to global historical interpretations and accentuating the separation of concrete reality into separate spheres – economic, social, political and cultural.

There are also the effects of the ideological crisis which have affected theoretical work during this transition from the previous historical period to the current one. The rejection of so-called overarching narratives and widespread adoption of the idea of a crisis of paradigms indicated that general analytical models were being abandoned in favour of postmodernism; the result was structures without history, history without a subject, theories without truth. It was truly the suicide of theory and of any attempt to produce a rational explanation of the world and of social relations.

Questions that are essential for any strategy for power, such as the nature of power itself, the state, strategies, alliances, the development of alternative blocs of forces, imperialism, foreign alliances, analyses of the balance of forces, the building of support, the development of a hegemonic bloc, and others, were either set aside or disappeared altogether. This was especially the case in so far as the social movements came to play the leading role in anti-neoliberal struggles. The passage from defensive struggles to a dispute over hegemony has to mean – as it does in the texts of the Comuna group or in the speeches of Hugo Chávez and Rafael Correa – a return to these questions, updating them for the period of neoliberal hegemony and the struggle against the tyranny of markets. Relying on mere denunciation, with no commitment to formulate and develop concrete political alternatives, tends to distance much of the intelligentsia from the concrete historical processes faced by the popular movements in the region. These, in turn, are condemned to endless processes of trial and error, because they do not have the support of a body of theory committed to the processes of change that really exist.

The opposite temptation is a strong one. Since Fidel Castro is not Lenin, Che is not Trotsky, Hugo Chávez is not Mao Zedong, Evo Morales is not Ho Chi Minh and Rafael Correa is not Gramsci, it might seem easier to reject the processes that really exist, because they do not correspond to the dreams of revolution cast in the image of another era, than to try to understand contemporary history as it is, with all its enigmas. In other words, either we recognize the signs left by the new Latin American mole, or we resign ourselves to the anthologies to which classic texts have been reduced by the nervous and sectarian hands of those who are afraid of history.

Taking refuge in classic texts is the most comfortable path, but also the surest route to failure. Defeats are usually attributed not to political causes but to moral ones. 'Betrayal' is the most common. The inability to give political explanations leads to sub-political, moral accounts. Trotsky's diagnosis of the Soviet Union is the opposite of this. It is a political, ideological, and social explanation of the course adopted by the Bolshevik leaders. For this reason it moves from the thesis of the revolution 'betrayed' to a substantive explanation of the state under bureaucratic hegemony.

The defence of principles supposedly contained in those classic texts seems to explain everything, except the most important thing: why is it that the doctrinaire, extremist views of the ultra-left never triumph, never manage to convince the majority of the population, never build organizations capable of leading revolutionary processes? They identify with the great balance sheets of defeats, but never lead to the growth of revolutionary political forces. Not by chance, their horizon is generally limited to polemics within the ultra-left itself and criticisms of other sections of the left, without leading big, national debates, without directly confronting the right or taking part in the dispute over hegemony. Those who only appear in public to criticize others on the left, often taking advantage of spaces in the right-wing media, have lost sight of who the main enemies are, and of the central confrontations with the right.

The challenge is to face the contradictions of history as it really exists, in the concrete conditions of Latin America today, and to tease out the elements with which to build a post-neoliberal order. The Comuna group were able to do this because they reread Bolivian history, particularly since the 1952 Revolution; deciphered its significance, identified the country's subsequent historical periods, understood the cycles that led to the decline of neoliberalism, managed to avoid the mistakes of the traditional left in relation to the historic subjects, and did the indispensable theoretical work needed to marry Evo Morales's leadership with the re-emergence of the indigenous movement as the essential protagonist of the current period of Bolivian history. In this way they were able to re-establish the link between theoretical and political practice and help the new popular movement to carry their economic and social demands into the ethnic and political arenas.

Such theoretical work is indispensable and can only be done on the basis of the concrete reality of each country, combined with reflection on the historical experiences and theories acquired by the popular movement over the years. Reality has no mercy on theoretical errors. Latin America in the twenty-first century needs and deserves a theory that is up to the challenges of the time.

REFORM AND/OR REVOLUTION

In recent decades, the Latin American left has oscillated between projects for reform and others projecting a rupture through armed struggle. The former were accused of being 'reformist', the latter of 'ultra-leftism' and 'adventurism'. To freeze the process of reforms without challenging the dominant system, without raising the question of power, is to drown in the reproduction of existing social and political relations. On the other hand, to concentrate on strategic demands without linking these to the underlying feelings and interests of the vast majority of the population leads to sectarianism, to positions that sound radical but are incapable of winning the hearts and minds of the people. Both versions have scored victories – social improvements for the poor, electoral triumphs in Cuba and Nicaragua – but by the beginning of the twenty-first century, in their original forms, both had had their day.

The movements that have been victorious since then are those that managed to escape the logic of these two opposed positions and combine both of them: they brought together a platform of reforms with modes of struggle that permitted the conquest of power. Trotsky's proposal in *The Transitional Programme* pointed in this direction, that is, to reforms that the dominant system is incapable of carrying out without suffering fatal consequences. These are, by definition, historical demands, subject to modification in time and space, which is why they are called 'transitional'; they serve to deepen the contradictions in the system and awaken society's awareness of them.

In practice, these demands have taken various forms: 'peace, bread and land' in Russia; expulsion of the Japanese invaders and agrarian revolution in China; the overthrow of the Batista dictatorship in Cuba; the expulsion of US invaders and reunification of the country in Vietnam; the overthrow of the Somoza dictatorship in Nicaragua. All had, nonetheless, a transitional character, pointing to the passage from capitalism to post-capitalism.

In Latin America, traditional reformism, which includes both the nationalist variety (particularly of Getúlio Vargas and Perón, in addition to the Mexican PRI) and the traditional left variety, which had two examples in Chile – the Popular Front in the 1930s and Popular Unity in the 1970s – remained at the level of reforms to the system, without linking these to the question of power. Apparently, Popular Unity raised the question of power when it proposed a transition, albeit gradual, from capitalism to socialism. However, as we shall see later, it did not analyse what would be the real conditions for defeating the existing power and building an alternative one. It believed these would emerge through the application of a programme of essentially economic reforms, as a natural consequence, and ended up falling into an economism that left it incapable of taking on other decisive centres of power, like the Armed Forces, imperialism and the private press.

The Cuban and Sandinista revolutions did manage to combine the struggle against dictatorship with the struggle against imperialism and, in the Cuban case, against capitalism too. Other examples of anti-dictatorial or merely democratic struggle concluded without projecting any strategy of rupture: witness the re-establishment of liberal-democratic systems in the Southern Cone of the continent. At the opposite extreme, some other struggles concentrated exclusively on the armed struggle, with its promise of a military rupture, and failed to connect with the sentiments or immediate needs of the vast majority of the population; they ended in isolation and defeat.

In the first case, the reforms got bogged down in the dominant system; in the second, they never managed to break out of the narrow circle of the organizations themselves, whether political or political-military in character.

Ever since the classic debate between Rosa Luxemburg and Eduard Bernstein, the left has been trapped in this dichotomy between reform and revolution. Bernstein laid everything on the movement, to the detriment of its final objectives, as if the accumulation of partial gains would pose and resolve the question of power and anti-capitalist transformation. Rosa Luxemburg drew attention to the fact that such reforms could open the way to a restructuring of capitalism, broadening its support – something Lenin called the 'labour aristocracy', in reference to the predominance of privileged layers within the working class.

The fact is that reformism acquired a dynamic of its own, and became hegemonic in the history of the left. Mainly this took the form of the social democratic parties coming to accept capitalism, or of the stageist strategies of the communist parties, which never managed to pass beyond the first of these stages and remained locked in reformism, with no rupture.

In Latin America, this was the principal face of the left, especially from the 1930s to the 1970s, in the midst of the industrial growth based on import substitution. In countries such as Mexico, Brazil and Argentina, such reformism was sponsored by nationalist forces led by the PRI, Vargas or Perón; in others, like Chile and Uruguay, it was articulated by an alliance of socialists and communists.

This logic – almost spontaneous within the left in a context of development and modernization – coincided with the expansion of the domestic, mass consumer market, the democratization of the public health and education systems and the growth of both urban and rural trade unions, which identified with aspects of this programme of democratic, anti-oligarchic and anti-imperialist reforms. As long as they served the needs of industrial expansion, they could be carried out. When the import substitution process went into decline, the alliance between the trade unions, sectors of the middle class and the industrial bourgeoisie broke down, rendering the reform strategy unviable. The Chilean experiment with Popular Unity was a solitary attempt to take this process further; now lacking any alliance with bourgeois sectors, it found itself smothered within the state apparatus and eventually defeated by a military coup supported by all of the bourgeoisie.

Nonetheless, the reformist logic survives, adapting to new political circumstances and driven by the spontaneous reaction of the popular movement to neoliberalism's attacks on its rights. It is important to take into account that the reappearance of reform projects occurs in a context where class relations have changed, with a much wider and deeper internationalization of the region's bourgeoisies and the erosion of formal labour rights, leading to a weakening of the workers' movement and the trade unions.

The current period presents a new challenge to the left's ability to overcome dichotomies that rather hinder than help the formulation of strategies linking theory and practice, concrete reality and strategic proposals. The processes which have triumphed in the past are rich in lessons of this ability, and have made those responsible – Lenin, Trotsky, Mao Zedong, Ho Chi Minh and Fidel Castro – the left's greatest strategists. In none of these cases did a reformist project simply transcend into a revolutionary one. Nor were any of them based on a pure proposal to break with capitalism in favour of socialism. All of them were born of concrete imperatives – to overthrow Tsarism, expel the invaders, revolt against dictatorship – but the leaderships of these struggles imposed a dynamic that went to the root of the problem and pointed to a rupture with the imperial system of domination and, with it, the underlying capitalist system.

Gramsci's description of the Russian Revolution as a revolution 'against *Capital*' has various meanings. One of them – which in the end had a tragic outcome – points to the fact that it occurred on the periphery of capitalism and faced the task of breaking out of its encirclement to enable the anticapitalist struggle in the most advanced countries to itself really negate and overcome capitalism. This objective was not achieved, neither in the crisis following the First World War, when the attempted revolutions in Germany were defeated and it was the far right that filled the void, nor later, when the USSR was left isolated and the revolutionary process moved in the opposite direction, towards the most backward countries of Asia.

Another of its meanings is that all revolutions are inevitably heterodox. No revolutionary formula has been repeated over time; all are unique and represent a peculiar combination of multiple factors. Such combinations mean that revolutions are always exceptions, never the rule, in historical development. The list of factors that make possible the outbreak of revolution include, according to Lenin, subjective and objective factors, which come together at a specific moment and for a limited time. The art of revolution is to harvest this combination of factors at just the right moment.

Lenin speaks of the revolutionary situation and the revolutionary crisis. The first occurs when there is such polarization in a country that those below are no longer prepared to live in the old way, and those above are no longer able to dominate in the old way. The revolutionary crisis occurs when a political leadership manages to steer this polarization towards a revolutionary outcome.

As Gramsci correctly pointed out, Lenin was referring to the strategy in backward societies, where the decisive axes of power come together in the state apparatus; seizing the latter should make it possible to dismantle this power and build a new one. In Gramscian terms, hegemony in these societies rests mainly on coercion rather than consensus. This analysis suggests that a much more complex political strategy would be required in societies where power rests on the fabrication of consensus and where the decisive axes of power are coordinated by the state, but exist mainly outside of it. Developing a strategy for power in these societies means developing alternative, hegemonic projects (counter-hegemonic ones), which end up contesting the state apparatus, but whose key battles will unfold in the complex fabric of economic, social and ideological relations in society as a whole.

The problem is that this proposition of Gramsci's seems to contradict one of the basic principles of Marxism, which states that, in class societies, 'the dominant ideas are those of the dominant class'. This is a structural condition, because ideology is not just the development of ideas on the cultural level: it is born deep within the process of capital accumulation, from the relations between capital and labour and the forms of appropriation of surplus value, from alienation as a fundamentally economic phenomenon that impregnates all social and cultural relations. The alienation we feel before the world we have ourselves created, but in which we do not recognize ourselves, comes from the relations of production, the process of wealth creation, which separates the products from the producers and prevents the latter from recognizing the wealth created by their labour.

This rupture between subject and object, between history and nature, between producer and product, between human beings and the world reproduces the mechanisms of alienation day after day, in every corner of society. It poses the question, both theoretical and political, of how, in these conditions, it is possible to develop a counter-hegemonic project, of how the hegemony of the dominant ideology can be broken. In other words, it presents a challenge: how can the alternative class bloc develop its own hegemony *before* it accedes to national, state, power?

Indeed, an alternative ideological force is essential for developing alternative political subjects. In Bolivia, for example, this was achieved through a reunification of political forces which assumed anew their indigenous identity. The victory in Bolivia – in this case an electoral one – was the result of a long and profound process of mobilization and struggle, over the previous half decade. Once it acceded to government, the development of an alternative project took a qualitative leap, for now it could mobilize more widely and employ more sophisticated instruments. But before it achieved this dominance, Bolivia's indigenous movement had to assume leadership, organizing and putting itself at the head of a bloc of alternative forces with a basic platform – nationalization of natural resources, agrarian reform, Constituent Assembly – and to demonstrate that this combination was possible. That meant understanding the real balance of forces, the dynamic of the confrontations, and the real strengths and weaknesses of each of the opposing blocs.

To comprehend better how counter-hegemonic projects can be developed, we need to look more closely at the two logics that have to be understood and overcome, so that we can then move on to the concrete analysis of concrete reality, with all its contradictions, structural determinations and potential for change.

The ultra-left logic

'Ultra-left' is a political category that has characterized much of the history of the international left. We are not going to rake over this history now; it is enough to mention Lenin's analysis in *'Left Wing' Communism: An Infantile Disorder* and Trotsky's in *Revolution and Counter-Revolution in Germany*, to take just two of the most rigorous and systematic critiques of this phenomenon.

The Russian Revolution, like all victorious revolutions, did not come about through calls for the overthrow of capitalism and the building of socialism. On the contrary, it captured the essential needs of the Russian people – for 'peace, bread and land' – and channelled these into a dynamic that ran up against not only Tsarism but also the alliances between Russia and the Western capitalist powers, and against capitalism itself. This is the art of revolutionary leadership: the ability to link immediate demands, or a minimum programme, with strategic objectives, or a maximum programme, thus opening the way to a revolutionary solution to the question of power. In other words, it means reconnecting, in a dynamic, non-segmented, non-corporative, and much less counterposed way, the terms 'reform' and 'revolution'.

Some on the ultra-left in Russia wanted to install socialism immediately and expropriate all sectors linked in one way or another to capitalism. They were opposed to the Brest-Litovsk agreement, by means of which the new Soviet government sought a kind of peaceful coexistence with Germany in order to begin rebuilding after the damage done by the war. They were also opposed to the New Economic Policy (NEP), introduced by Lenin to encourage the reactivation of small and medium rural landholdings and to restore production and supply to the domestic market, especially in the towns. The aim of the NEP had been to combat the threat of widespread hunger resulting from the encirclement of the countryside, where the counter-revolution of the Whites was prolonged by intervention from more than fifteen foreign armies and by the failure of the revolution in Germany, which, if successful, could have broken the siege and isolation of the Bolshevik government.

Immediately after the triumph of the revolution, a system of 'war communism' was decreed, which simply shared out what there was in the most egalitarian way possible, as it were socializing the existing poverty. When the war ended, there was strong internal pressure to re-establish economic growth and ensure the supply of basic necessities, especially to the cities. It was to this end, and in a defensive situation, that the government decreed the NEP. For the ultra-left, it was a betrayal of revolutionary ideals, a capitulation by Lenin, Trotsky and their fellow revolutionaries. The correctness of the policy became clear a few years later, when the change in policy carried out by Stalin failed to resolve the question of the countryside, the peasants intensified their supply boycott and the new leadership of the revolution had to resort to the worst possible solution: the expropriation of the land by force and the death of millions of peasants from starvation. Unresolved, the agrarian question was removed from the agenda through the front door, only to come back through the window in explosive fashion, marking one of the weak points of the Russian Revolution. Right up to the last days of the USSR, this was an issue that was never resolved.

The ultra-left has difficulty understanding defeats, retreats and negative shifts in the balance of forces. It tends to reduce its diagnoses to accusations of betrayal by the leaders, generally discovering innumerable cases of leaderships that have become corrupt or bureaucratized, and which have reneged on their ideals or platforms. But critical balance sheets that do not lead to alternatives also fail to build support for their positions; they end up being a part of the defeat, because they do not translate into solutions.

The crises unleashed by the First World War confirmed Lenin's prediction, when he said that it was never more difficult to make a revolution than at the beginning of a war, when chauvinism holds sway and demands national unity against other countries, but it was never more likely than in the course of a war. When the inter-imperialist character of the war became clear, people could see that they were being used as canon fodder in a conflict that didn't concern them. In Germany and Italy, however, the possibility of revolution that arose from the suffering and defeat of war never came to fruition – the attempts failed, leaving the way clear for the mass counter-revolutions of fascism and Nazism to impose their solutions to the crisis.

In Germany, a failure to grasp the strength and danger of Nazism meant that the social democratic and communist parties did not put unity against this enemy above their own differences. They thereby facilitated the rise of Hitler, who repressed them all. The communists called the social democrats 'social fascists' – socialists in word, fascists in deed – and argued that they would open the door to Nazism. The socialists accused the communists of being an extension of Soviet totalitarianism, something quite similar to Nazism. Trotsky drew up a scathing balance sheet of the ultra-leftist attitudes of both parties. They were incapable of understanding that Nazism was the enemy of all the left; they underestimated its strength and facilitated its rise.

More recently, we saw typical examples of ultra-leftist positions in China, during the Cultural Revolution, and in Cambodia, soon after the defeat of the United States in Vietnam. China disagreed with the Soviet attitude to the building of socialism and relations with US imperialism; it claimed that the USSR was restoring capitalism, citing as an example of adaptation to capitalist lifestyles the importing of a car factory from Fiat in Italy – located in a city now renamed Togliatti, in homage to the former leader of the Italian Communist Party. According to this analysis, as a major capitalist power in an imperialist epoch, the Soviets must also be a new imperialist power, like the US. While the United States represented decadent imperialism, the USSR was characterized as a rising power; it was therefore more dangerous and should be targeted as the main enemy.

On this basis, the Chinese did all they could to combat the

USSR and all those forces and governments that seemed to depend on its support. They went so far as to back racist or dictatorial governments in South Africa and Chile, because these opposed so-called Soviet expansionism. They classified the Cuban government as 'the armed wing of Soviet imperialism', because it helped the Angolans to resist the South African invasion.

The logic of the Chinese position – often repeated by others on the ultra-left – was that if they didn't displace the USSR from its position, China would never have room to expand its own leadership in the world. Hence the violence of the repeated attacks on the Soviets and – as also happened with other forces that adopted a similar position – the alliance with decadent imperialism (the United States) to try to liquidate the main enemy (the Soviet Union). This alliance, sealed with Richard Nixon's visit to China, gave rise to the so-called ping-pong diplomacy.

To cap it all, despite the immense defeat it would have meant for the first socialist revolution in history to restore capitalism and become an imperialist power, China continued to preach that the revolution was advancing and that imperialism was a 'paper tiger', calling on peoples everywhere to rebel and change the world, as if nothing had happened.

Cambodia saw one of the most tragic examples of sectarianism by a left-wing government. This put into practice an even more radical version of the Chinese Cultural Revolution's diagnosis that capitalism, its culture and its cities, corrupt human beings, in contrast with the pure life of the countryside. Millions of people were sent off to become proletarianized on the land, and many were eventually executed. Driven by a dogmatic and sectarian vision of capitalist ideology and modern culture, the Cambodian regime carried out a brutal form of ideological 'cleansing' until it was overthrown with the aid of the Vietnamese, who had already suffered invasion by China, on the grounds that they had become agents of the Soviet Union.

The most radical currents of the left – among them Trotskyists and Maoists – are characterized by their criticisms of the majority, reformist currents. They have always tended to adopt this critical view, without ever being able to develop mass support – most typically in the case of the Trotskyists. In the intellectual field, more understandably, such critical tendencies have played an important part, pointing out the mistakes and 'deviations' of the political forces. However, precisely because of this intellectual character (they are not themselves a political force), they are unable to formulate alternatives that would overcome the problems they identify, even when their diagnoses turn out to be correct. Often, these critical views arise from a contrast with what are regarded as the principles of revolutionary theory; at other times, from what are seen as the internal inconsistencies of the projects in question. Such currents make a key contribution to political practice, but they often succumb to the temptation of ultra-leftism because they put theory before the concrete conditions of struggle, which prevents them from grasping the dilemmas imposed by concrete practice.

What is the contemporary logic of ultra-leftism, which is so widely disseminated in these times when liberalism has such an ability to co-opt, and there is such a contradiction between the historic decline of capitalism and the retreat of socialism as a current possibility?

In quite a thorough text, James Petras – one of the most important representatives of these ultra-left positions – sets out to analyse the history of the left in order to explain the present and future of revolutionary politics;[4] his text was in response to an article that Perry Anderson wrote in 2000 to inaugurate a new phase of the *New Left Review*, the journal he had begun to edit forty years earlier. In that article, Anderson had compared the situation at the beginning of the new century with that which existed when he took over the publication.[5]

---

4. James Petras, 'Notes toward an understanding of revolutionary politics today', *Links: International Journal of Socialist Renewal* 19, May–August 2001.

5. Perry Anderson, 'Renewals', *New Left Review* 1, January–February 2000.

In line with the logic underlying his approach, Petras includes a number of extremely aggressive references in his article, seeking to brand Perry Anderson as one of those intellectuals who had adopted 'a certain apolitical centrism', born of defeatism, the self-flagellation of the left and its capitulation before the strength of neoliberalism. This language matches the content of Petras's argument and that of others who take a similar stance: the dismissal of those criticized is justified because they have abandoned the left, capitulated, and because they defend views that are only apparently of the left. Therefore they need to be not just answered but thoroughly thrashed and 'unmasked', to make sure they no longer exert a negative influence within the left.

But what *was* Anderson's balance sheet in 2000? In making his comparison between that period and the 1960s, Anderson organized the differences into three categories: historical, intellectual and cultural.

In the 1960s, 'a third of the planet had broken with capitalism'. While Nikita Khrushchev proposed reforms in the USSR, China maintained its prestige, the Cuban Revolution was unfolding in the Americas, the Vietnamese were successfully resisting US occupation and capitalism felt under threat. Intellectually, there began 'a discovery process of suppressed leftist and Marxist traditions', and 'alternative strands of revolutionary Marxism' gained currency.[6] Culturally, compared with the conformist atmosphere of the 1950s, rock music and new wave cinema provided a flavour of rebellion.

Four decades later, the climate could not have been more different. 'The Soviet bloc has disappeared. Socialism has ceased to be a widespread ideal. Marxism is no longer dominant in the culture of the left.' The 1990s brought 'the virtually uncontested consolidation, and universal diffusion of neoliberalism'.[7]

Five interconnected processes had radically changed the landscape:

6. Anderson, 'Renewals', p. 7.
7. Ibid., pp. 9–10.

1) US capitalism reasserted its predominance in all fields (economic, political, military and cultural);

2) European social democracy made a turn towards neoliberalism;

3) Japanese capitalism entered a deep and prolonged recession, while China moved towards membership in the WTO, and India, for the first time in its history, came to depend on the IMF;

4) The new Russian economy did not provoke popular protest, in spite of the catastrophic regression imposed on the country;

5) The deep socio-economic changes imposed by neoliberalism were accompanied by two shifts, one political and the other military:

- ideologically, the neoliberal consensus extended to parties identifying with the 'third way', like Tony Blair's Labour Party in Britain and Bill Clinton's Democrats in the United States; with this, it seemed the 'single orthodoxy' and the Washington Consensus had become immovable, because a change of government in either of neoliberalism's main bastions would no longer change the model, but simply reproduce it;
- militarily, the war in the Balkans ushered in the age of 'humanitarian wars', a type of military intervention conducted in the name of 'human rights'.

Among intellectuals, who had previously been mostly socialist, there were two main reactions. The first was conversion to the new order – capitalism passed from being a necessary evil to become 'a necessary and on balance salutary social order',[8] with the superiority of private enterprise given pride of place. The second was consolation – the need to sustain a message of hope led here to overestimating the importance of the various forms of opposition, as if it were these that set the tone of the period.

---

8. Ibid., p. 13.

As a result, the idea 'of the spread of democracy as a substitute for socialism, either as hope or claim', became widely accepted. It didn't seem to matter that the actual practice of democracy had been emptied of all content, limiting its historical horizons to what currently existed – the liberal democracy and capitalist economy as promoted by Francis Fukayama. Faced with this situation, Anderson concluded that:

> The only starting-point for a realistic Left today is a lucid registration of historical defeat ... No collective agency able to match the power of capital is yet on the horizon ... For the first time since the Reformation, there are no longer any significant oppositions – that is, systematic rival outlooks – within the thought-world of the West ... neo-liberalism as a set of principles rules undivided across the globe: the most successful ideology in world history.[9]

The whole system of references in which the generation of the 1960s had been educated, had now been swept from the map.

Anderson's analysis completes his 1994 account of neoliberalism, which remains the best overview of the new hegemonic project.[10] Already at that time, he drew attention to the breadth and depth of this model, which introduced radical changes in the Keynesian model and extended market relations to areas never before reached by capitalism, like the ex-socialist countries, including the USSR, Eastern Europe and China. The model launched by the far right proceeded to incorporate first nationalists and then social democrats. It was possible to say: 'We are all neo-liberals now'.[11]

It is against this analysis that James Petras reacts so strongly, in a denunciation that tries to interpret the history of the left without, as he sees it, succumbing to the liberal illusion and defeatism. According to him, 'During periods of counter-

9. Ibid., pp. 16–17.

10. Perry Anderson, 'Introduction' to *Mapping the West European Left*, London 1994.

11. This remark is an inversion of Milton Friedman's claim in a 1965 letter to *Time* magazine, later attributed to Richard Nixon, that 'we are all Keynesians now'.

revolutionary ascendancy, following temporary or historic defeats, many of the former radical intellectuals revert to their class origins, discovering the virtues of right-wing ideologies', which, he says, they present as invincible and irreversible. They make the mistake of concentrating on a 'particular one-dimensional configuration of contemporary power as the reality', in an approach without historical roots.[12]

Petras sets out to debunk a certain view that sees the 1950s as dominated by conformism, the two following decades by the spread of revolution, and the period from 1980 to 2000 as one of defeat and dissolution. He recounts a series of struggles in the 1950s, none of them fundamental, to try to show that there were mobilizations – but this does not alter the general picture of capitalist stability, albeit uneven.

As ever, the left finds it difficult to recognize political defeats and setbacks. The 1950s unquestionably saw US hegemony reach its height. Eric Hobsbawm has characterized the long cycle of growth stretching from the end of the Second World War to the mid 1970s as 'the golden age of capitalism',[13] when the three locomotives of metropolitan capitalism, the United States, Germany and Japan, found their economic growth synchronized. The fact that the second two countries achieved this status is itself noteworthy, after being destroyed in the Second World War and then rebuilt, along with the Italian economy, with the help of the US-financed Marshall Plan. This coincided with growth in peripheral capitalist countries like Brazil, Argentina and Mexico, as well as in non-capitalist areas, which ended up contributing to growth rates under the hegemony of the world capitalist market.

Hobsbawm believes that, in the 1950s, the United States established its economic and technological superiority over the USSR in irreversible fashion, but that the full effects of this were only felt a decade or two later. Drawing on Second World War rearmament, the US economy was already

---

12. Petras, 'Introduction' to 'Notes toward an understanding of revolutionary politics today'.
13. Eric Hobsbawm, *Age of Extremes*, London 1994, esp. Chapter 9.

recovering from the 1929 crisis by the end of the 1930s and experienced growth in the 1940s, while Europe and Japan were destroyed.

Whatever the important struggles that can be identified in the 1950s, what is needed is to take the measure of the hegemony in the period, and not limit one's view to the strength of anti-hegemonic forces. For Petras, 'it is a monstrous distortion to refer to the 1950s as a period of 'conformity'"[14] – yet he fails to grasp that this was a period of considerable ideological consensus around 'the American way of life'.

He refers to political developments that might contradict Anderson's argument: the presence of powerful communist parties in Greece, Italy, France and Yugoslavia; the revolts in Hungary, Poland and East Germany; the re-emergence of the left in Britain and the United States; the Vietnamese victory against the French in 1954; and, what he sees as steps toward the following decade, the support for the war in Algeria and the peasant struggles that led to the revolutions in Cuba and Indochina.

These are clearly insufficient counterweights to the immense stabilization and consolidation of capitalist hegemony that characterized the decade. The procedure is typically ultraleft: it takes a few examples, without measuring their relative importance in the overall balance of forces. A political analysis of any given situation cannot limit itself to examples of the supposed strength of the left. A political analysis which is not merely descriptive, which has a serious journalistic or academic function, and aims to elucidate the big class confrontations, must concentrate on the balance of forces while understanding that any balance of forces is temporary, referring as it does to the relationship between the strength of one side and that of the other.

In this sense, it is impossible to overlook the strengthening of the Western bloc and the reaffirmation of US leadership, alongside the reconstruction on more modern foundations

---

14. Petras, Section 1 of 'Notes toward an understanding of revolutionary politics today'.

of Germany, Japan and Italy, all of them led by conservative forces.

This inability to characterize a decade in accordance with its dominant aspects is patently obvious in the way Petras rushes to deny Anderson's contrast between the relative conformism of the 1950s and the radicalization of the decade that followed. For Petras, 'If the 1950s were not a period of worldwide conformity, neither were the 1960s, in all of their manifestations, an age of uniform revolutionary upheaval.'[15] Historical development is based, fundamentally, on uneven processes. No period can be described as homogeneously moving in one direction or the other. It is therefore inappropriate to apply the word 'uniformly' to any historical period.

Petras recognizes the rise of mass struggles in North America, Europe and parts of the Third World, but holds that there were important setbacks in important countries and various contradictions and conflicts within the mass movements. He argues that the result should be a positive re-evaluation and a creative development of Marxist thought to take in new areas and new problems.

He places particular importance on the struggles in Indochina, Cuba and other countries where peasant struggles gave rise to new strategic ideas. However, he says that much intellectual work contributed little politically, because it failed to grasp the role of imperialism in the contemporary world. He dismisses the counter-cultural movements of the 1960s as motors of individualism, which were finally co-opted by 'market populism' – they were so permeated by drugs, according to him, that 'opium became the opium of the left'.

For Petras, 'There are links between some variants of intellectual and cultural life in the 1960s and 1970s and the right turn in the 1990s: the substantive differences in political activity in the two periods, particularly in the Anglo-Saxon world, are bridged by the pseudo-radical individualist cultural practices and values in both periods.'[16]

---

15. Ibid.
16. Ibid.

The key to the problem is presented as a deep division between anti-imperialist thinkers and Western Marxists. The latter had supposedly denied the importance of the struggles in Indochina, Latin America and South Africa, giving a derogatory connotation to the expression Third World, while focusing their attention on the central capitalist countries. The theoreticians of anti-imperialism, for their part, had focused their attention on the relations between centre and periphery, sometimes from an abstract, globalist perspective, as with Samir Amin, Andre Gunder Frank and Immanuel Wallerstein, and sometimes from a perspective of class struggle.

On the other hand, military coups in Brazil and Indonesia, supported by the United States, had interrupted two processes in the biggest and most promising countries of the Third World. Petras also includes, in this category of 'counter-revolution in the revolution', the turn in China, which opened the way to what would become capitalist restoration at the end of the 1970s. At the same time, Khrushchev's anti-Stalinist movement had been defeated by the 'repressive apparatus'.

Petras's inability to grasp the global correlation of forces is revealed most clearly in the passage to a decade of obvious reversals for the popular camp and of obvious gains for imperialism – the 1990s. He takes it up in a section of the essay entitled, 'Restoration, imperialism and revolution in the 1990s', in which the inclusion of the third element aims to reinforce its presence even in a decade like this.

His main claim in relation to this new period is that 'certainly only an ahistorical and hasty judgement can claim that the decade was a period of unprecedented historical defeats, surpassing anything in prior history'. He compares this period with another, from the beginning of the 1930s to the beginning of the 1940s, in which he says there was huge setback and devastation of the left in Europe on an unprecedented scale, either through physical repression, isolation or co-option. Nothing similar, he argues, had occurred in the 1990s:

US 'hegemony', a rather vacuous concept that inflates the role of 'political persuasion', is totally inappropriate when one considers the scope and depth of violence in the recent past and its continuous use on a selective but demonstrable basis in the present.[17]

In this way, Petras calculates shifts in the balance of forces as a function of the level of repression, and not in terms of imperialism's hegemonic capacity, which is a synthesis of both force and persuasion. If the two periods mentioned are, in many ways, not comparable, it is nonetheless clear that Petras underestimates the scale of the imperialist victory in the new period, which began in the 1990s.

The years from 1930 to 1940 saw the USSR grow stronger, and liberalism grow weaker as a result of the Great Depression; the second successive war in Europe, as an inter-imperialist war, attacked the foundations of European capitalism and created the conditions for the left to grow, just as the struggle by the communist parties against fascism and Nazism consolidated the international prestige of the USSR.

Thus, the defensive position the left had to adopt in this period – expressed especially by the VII Congress of the Communist International, which approved Dimitrov's resolutions on the anti-fascist united front – although it had a strategic character, did not come about in a context of political and ideological dismantling of the left like that which occurred in the 1990s.

When Petras lists the movements of resistance to neoliberalism, he misses out the main thing: the fundamental, strategic changes that happened at the beginning of the 1990s, with all the consequences these had. I am referring to the shift from a bipolar world to a unipolar one, under US hegemony, and the shift from Keynesianism to the neoliberal model. The combination of both and their consequences – of which the most important is the hegemony of the North 'American way of life', as a value and as a lifestyle – give a globally regressive character to the new period. Whatever counter-tendencies

---

17. Ibid., Section 3.

there may be, these do not outweigh the negative shift in the balance of forces.

The disappearance of the bipolar world does not just mean a shift to a world under the hegemony of a single, imperialist super-power. It also means an ever larger gap between the strength of the United States and that of other powers. At the same time as the world's number two power, the USSR, disappeared, the economies of Japan and Germany were stagnating. And because the strength of a country is defined not in comparison with its past achievements, but in relation to the strength of other countries, the United States entered the new period stronger than ever before.

The consequences for the left were devastating. There was an ideological retreat, with a questioning of everything that had to do with socialism (state, party, labour, planning, socialization, etc.), and a political one too, with social democracy sliding to the right, the break-up of alliances with the communist parties, the weakening of both these and the trade unions, and a proliferation of right-wing governments. Any global evaluation of the 1990s must conclude that there was a radical change in the correlation of forces between the blocs. The disappearance of the USSR and the socialist camp saw these replaced, not with something further to the left, but with the restoration of capitalism in its neoliberal form. Socialism, which had been a part of history through most of the twentieth century, practically disappeared, to be replaced by anti-neoliberal struggle. Capitalism extended its hegemony as never before in history.

A comparison of the 1990s with the present decade in Latin America also confirms the regressive nature of the former. It was only at the end of that decade that the first anti-neoliberal government emerged in the region, that of Venezuela. Although there were varied forms of resistance to neoliberalism, these developed in a defensive framework. But it was only the strength accumulated in this defensive phase that made possible the current hegemonic struggle, marking a new, more favourable situation for the popular camp.

The ultra-left view does not take account of these setbacks, rather clinging to one of its constant themes, the permanent possibility of revolution. The only option this leaves is to accuse the political leaders of 'betrayal', making them responsible for the fact the revolution hasn't happened. Originally, this line of analysis goes back to Trotsky. He held that the objective conditions for revolution already existed, and it was precisely such betrayal by leaders that created the obstruction; the problem was that these leaderships had become bureaucratized, defended their own interests, made compromises with the ruling class and abandoned the side of the revolution and the left.

This kind of analysis is also based on what Lenin said about the 'aristocracy of labour': a section of the working class that identifies with colonial and/or imperial domination and forms the social basis for certain kinds of political representation.

Nonetheless, we need to take account of alterations in the balance of forces that indicate changes in the objective conditions, especially in the current period. Here there is a contradictory combination between setbacks in the subjective conditions for anti-capitalist struggle and the evident limits of capitalism. The victory of the imperialist camp and the defeat of the socialist camp, along with the structural and ideological changes introduced by neoliberal policies, have changed the objective and subjective conditions for political struggle. This is how the possibilities for struggle should be understood, in their actual historical context, and not by applying the same rigid and dogmatic approach to all situations.

More recently, before Evo Morales had even assumed office, Petras was already accusing him of betrayal, and calling Álvaro García Linera a 'neoliberal intellectual', which shows a failure to understand the concrete conditions of the Bolivian process. Leaders of other countries, and even the leadership of the MST in Brazil, were not spared similar accusations.

What does the charge of 'betrayal' imply? Could it be a question of ideological co-option? This would give it a concrete class meaning, and a perfectly plausible one, given the way institutional politics works, the reach of neoliberalism's ideological values in today's world and the pressure from powerful, private media.

The worst consequence of this type of criticism is that it tends to foster the idea that the 'traitor' is the main enemy, a representative of the 'new right' who needs to be 'unmasked', defeated and destroyed. Otherwise, the new force represented by these criticisms cannot become an alternative leadership for the left.

The results of such a political approach have been isolation and a blurring of the boundaries between the left and the right. This has produced a sense of impotence, reflecting the absence of movements with these positions that have been able to build major forces and lead revolutions. Victorious movements like the 26 July Movement in Cuba, the Sandinista Front in Nicaragua, Bolivarianism in Venezuela or the Movement to Socialism (MAS) in Bolivia, even when they call for radical forms of struggle as in Cuba and Nicaragua, mainly adopt a broad political approach, in their platforms and slogans as well as in their alliances. What characterizes them as revolutionary movements is the fact that they manage to tackle the question of power in a direct, concrete and appropriate way, and to build a strategic force that corresponds to the history of popular struggles in their country and to the kind of power structures that exist there.

The particular experience in Chile, where the Popular Unity government of Salvador Allende sought a peaceful transition to socialism, presented the revolutionary left with a tricky dilemma. Ever since it was founded, the Movement of the Revolutionary Left (MIR) had a class vision of the state as bourgeois, denounced the pro-imperialist character of the national bourgeoisies and therefore saw as impossible an institutional road to socialism. Nonetheless, after Allende's unexpected election in 1970, it had to decide what position to take.

In line with its strategic orientation, immediately after Popular Unity's electoral victory the MIR offered to provide personal protection for Allende, forming what was called the Group of Friends of the President (GAP). In this capacity, it sought to investigate the first act of destabilization carried out by those who would later stage the Chilean coup – namely the kidnapping and murder of the then commander-in-chief of the Armed Forces, General René Schneider. He had Christian Democratic tendencies and had been appointed by Eduardo Frei, the president who was still serving out his time in office. His killing had been immediately blamed on armed movements of the left, but the investigations discovered it was a plot by the right, seeking to provoke tension and spread fears that under Allende the armed groups would act openly. The objective was to prevent the Chilean Congress from ratifying the victory of Allende – who had won with just 36.3 per cent of the vote in the first round, and who therefore, according to the Constitution, had to be confirmed by parliament.

The challenges faced by a government coming to power in circumstances like those in which Salvador Allende was elected – with a radical, anti-capitalist programme, but without the support of even a simple majority of the population – were complex. Allende tried to carry out his political platform, but found himself smothered within the state apparatus, until he was eventually overthrown by a military coup. The MIR fought for a strict and even more radical application of the socialist programme. On the one hand, they were convinced that the existing power structures would prevent the application of this programme, and therefore considered a military coup inevitable. On the other, they did their utmost to have the programme implemented as deeply as possible.

The MIR succeeded in spreading the organization of the popular movement, especially in the countryside, in the shanty towns and among students; in alliance with more radical sections of the Socialist Party, they proposed and began to build organs of popular power, as the structures of what might become an alternative national power. Since they regarded a military coup as inevitable, they tried to prepare the mass movement and the party itself to confront this. They believed that, once the reformist strategy had had its opportunity and failed, then the time would come for a revolutionary strategy.

The military coup did indeed happen, and it hit the whole of the left hard. It represented not just a failure for the reformist strategy, but a brutal change for the worse in the balance of forces. It also meant the beginning of a strategy of annihilation against the entire left and popular movement, with the MIR as its main target. A mistaken judgement about what was possible at the time of Allende's victory led them to deepen the level of confrontation, without the left being in a position to prevent the coup or successfully to resist it once it began. The course of events could have been different, if there had been a rethinking of the relation between reforms and revolution and an attempt to carry out projects of urban and agrarian reform. Even if these had not had a directly anti-capitalist nature, they would have represented a profound social and democratic advance, in the direction of anti-capitalism. The MIR's slogan – 'Socialism is not a few factories and some land for the people, but all the factories and all the land' – reflected this maximalism. This was the most important organization of the revolutionary left in Chile, with an extraordinary membership that demonstrated tremendous political creativity and organizational ability. Yet it succumbed to this ultra-left logic.

The question below is posed as an updating of the relation between reform and revolution, and of the relations between radical, anti-capitalist movements and centre-left forces with a different orientation. What position should a radical organization adopt in relation to governments like those of Lula, Tabaré Vázquez, Cristina Kirchner, Daniel Ortega, José Luis Rodríguez Zapatero, and others of the kind? These are not governments of the right; in all these countries, there are indeed forces of the right, that act in opposition to these governments, even though they are not carrying out a clearly left-wing programme.

Manichaeism is an all too familiar phenomenon in politics. In such situations, it pushes on the one hand towards a subordinate alliance, in an effort to occupy what space exists to the left, and on the other hand towards the creation of new spaces, in an effort to break this logic. Manichaeism also entails the serious and permanent risk of concentrating one's attacks on the government – of the centre-left, now characterized as the 'new right' – and thereby promoting confusion instead of strengthening the polarization between right and left. The failure to recognize the left or centre-left character of the governments mentioned tends to disorient the forces that seek to occupy the space to their left. By centring their opposition on these governments themselves, they end up benefiting the right. What they should do instead is take a position on specific policies, supporting those that have a left character and opposing the right-wing ones.

If a political approach loses sight of where the right is located and of the dangers it poses, when it confuses a moderate, contradictory ally with the enemy, this shows it hasn't grasped the reality of the existing political landscape. This is what happened to the German Communist Party. When it characterized German social democracy at the beginning of the 1930s as a disguised form of fascism, an ally of fascism or as a part of the right, it was mistaking a vacillating ally for the enemy. It couldn't differentiate between the sides, wasted energies that should have been directed against the dangerous rise of the right, isolated itself and effectively assisted the victory of the enemy. The same thing happened in reverse, dramatically and tragically, with German social democracy. By characterizing the Communist Party as a different version of Nazi totalitarianism, the Stalinist version, it completed the division that helped the Nazis come to power and then repress both social democrats and communists without distinction.

If we take the case of the Lula government, its own contradictory character left it open to praise and criticism from both the right and the left, in spite of the great differences between them.

The left should be working to open up an area of political and ideological dispute in which the polarization between right and left is what predominates. This is not out of some fetish, but because one side represents the maintenance and reproduction of the system, while the left is seeking to create an anti-neoliberal and anti-capitalist alternative. Ideological and social struggle should be pursued with vigour, but they must be subordinate to the political struggle, which is key, and whose focus is opposition to the dominant power and the building of an alternative power.

The left experiences that have managed to develop sufficient strength to win the struggle for hegemony are those that have shown themselves able to develop mass struggles and the battle of ideas, while keeping the political dispute as their main reference. This means that the ideological battle must choose the decisive strategic themes that are capable of uniting all the popular forces at a given moment – which is at present that of anti-neoliberal and post-neoliberal struggle. It is anti-neoliberal in the sense of combating all forms of submission to the market; it is post-neoliberal in the sense that it promotes alternatives centred on the public sphere, because in the neoliberal era conflict is based on a polarization between the market sphere and the public sphere.

Doctrinaire logic subordinates everything to the ideological struggle, and sets itself up as the guardian of Marxist principles and their theoretical purity. As a result, it not only remains isolated but also creates even bigger divisions within the left, over interpretations of theory – Trotskyism, for example. It also tends to decry all new revolutionary experiences which, since they are always heterodox, 'against *Capital*', have to be rejected and condemned. This is what happened with all the victorious revolutionary processes, in Russia, China, Cuba, Vietnam, Nicaragua, and it is happening today with Venezuela, Bolivia and Ecuador. It is similar to what happened in France in 1968, when Sartre wrote of the difficulties the communists had in recognizing the new forms of the class struggle – what he called their 'fear of revolution' as it actually existed, which was inevitably different from the Bolsheviks' assault on the Winter Palace.

The Russian Revolution, for example, could not represent a break with capitalism, because that would contradict Marx's prediction that socialism would arise in the countries of the capitalist heartland. The Chinese Revolution should confine itself to expelling the invaders and developing a national capitalism. The Cuban Revolution was explicitly condemned for using methods considered 'adventurist' and 'provocative', when the conditions supposedly did not exist for the kind of rupture that was being proposed. In none of them, including the Venezuelan and Bolivian processes, did the working class play a leading part, nor did the economic circumstances make it possible to speak of anti-capitalism.

However, the truth is concrete: it is born out of the concrete analysis of concrete reality. Principles are principles: they do not move out of books into reality, but are concretely reborn out of daily struggles when they demonstrate their usefulness. Theoretical mistakes cost dear in practice; but theoretical zeal cannot confine the rich experience of concrete historical processes in narrow, dogmatic bands.

Álvaro García Linera's analysis of the way the traditional left in Bolivia regarded the indigenous population is an excellent contemporary example of how concrete reality rebels against dogma. The Bolivian left always sought to develop a workers and peasants' alliance along the lines of the Bolshevik Revolution. There was concrete support for this in the existence of a mining proletariat, located in a key sector of the Bolivian economy, which could exert a kind of veto power over the country's economic activity, because paralysing the mines meant shutting down the entire economy. However the isolation of such an enclave, not least physically, made it difficult to develop an alternative hegemonic project led by the miners.

The role of the miners in the 1952 Revolution, with the nationalization of the tin mines, the development of workers' councils, even the replacement of the Armed Forces by self-defence brigades, gave the impression that the miners did have such a strategic capacity. The agrarian reform, in turn, seemed to suggest the peasantry could be a strategic ally for the mining proletariat, in classic style. It was an attempt to apply to a specific, concrete reality, a theoretical scheme derived from another reality – the Soviet one.

The rural population was viewed in terms of its labour, and the forms of reproduction of its conditions of existence. Since they lived on the land, they were classified as peasants, regardless of whether they were indigenous or not. They were to forget their ancient origins and play the part of the peasants, subordinate allies of the mine workers – and up to a point vacillating allies too, since they were not proletarianized but still tied to their smallholdings. The economic determination was seen as direct and mechanical, reducing indigenous peoples to peasants.

It was the specific, concrete reconstruction of Bolivian history, beginning in the pre-colonial period, that allowed García Linera to grasp the decisive elements of the native peoples' identity, of their indigenous condition – more specifically their condition as Aymara, Quechua or Guaraní. It was this kind of analysis that made it possible to grasp the identity of the indigenous peoples as a whole, that allowed them to assume this identity politically and elect Evo Morales as president, as well as to build a party – the MAS – as a vehicle to establish their hegemony over Bolivian society as a whole.

One case where a victorious strategy was apparently repeated was that of the Sandinista Revolution in relation to the Cuban Revolution. It was an exceptional situation, but it deserves to be noted. There were, it is true, differences in the way these guerrilla wars were conducted, and in the much broader way in which the Nicaraguan experience incorporated women, Christians, children and old people into the clandestine mass struggle. But in essence, the similarities between these two processes, occurring in the same historical period, are greater than those between any other revolutionary experiences. If the element of surprise was decisive in Cuba, in Nicaragua it was a combination of the US defeat in Vietnam, the struggles against the war and for civil rights at home, the Watergate crisis and Richard Nixon's resignation, that led to Jimmy Carter's efforts to restore US prestige abroad. Through a policy of human rights, he sought to distance Washington from the dictatorships it had previously supported in the continent.

Guerrilla movements in Guatemala and El Salvador were, however, unable to repeat the experience. One decisive factor prevented this and pushed the guerrillas back into political forms of struggle: the international balance of forces had changed and made it impossible for armed struggle to prevail. Whatever the criticisms of the left's current experiences, that alternative is no longer available. It means that the left has to settle accounts with the existing power structures, reworking the radical critique which would allow it to go beyond these structures while passing through them.

The shift to the current historical period has created new parameters for struggle. The strategy of reforms leading to a violent break through armed struggle is no longer an option. This should make it easier to once more develop rich and concrete combinations between reform and revolution.

The reformist logic

The reformist logic underestimates or abandons both the ideological struggle and the mass struggle. It seeks the lines of least resistance, to advance where it can, in an attempt to gradually change the balance of forces without touching on the central question of the relations of power. Undoubtedly it achieved significant advances in Latin America – especially under the nationalist governments in Argentina, Mexico and Brazil – when the industrial bourgeoisie's plans for economic development coincided with those of the trade union movement and sectors of the middle classes. These were the decades of rapid growth, with income distribution and upward social mobility, which came to an end when the long expansive wave of international and Latin American capital went into decline.

In theory, the reformist project seeks a profound overhaul of the existing economic, social and political structures. It obeys a logic of spontaneous, progressive change, of successive shifts in the power relations, won through economic and social demands that gradually strengthen the popular camp and undermine the enemy pole.

This has been and remains the prevailing logic in the immense majority of historical situations. The conditions required for a revolutionary process to emerge are much more unusual, and have to be combined in very particular ways to make a revolution – that special historical moment – possible. The spontaneous ideology and practice of social, economic and political struggles are those of gradually winning improvements in the situation of the mass of the people, through gradual changes in existing legislation and through gradually conquering greater space in the existing political institutions.

Although reformism has been responsible for most of the economic and social gains won over the decades, it has failed as a strategy to transform, little by little, the relations of power. Its attempt to turn partial victories into qualitative changes in the relations of power, and thereby to introduce a new political system, never bore fruit. Indeed, the reforms were neither a substitute for revolution, nor did they lead to revolution; all too often they did not even succeed in toning down the reaction of the ruling classes to such moderate, gradualist proposals from the left. This failure was mainly a result of not making the question of power the central concern, and therefore not working to develop alternative forms of power. This deficiency is decisive, and fatal for any political force aiming at structural transformation. It is an issue that often goes unnoticed, only to return with much greater force and take unawares those who propose changes to the prevailing power relations – and the less prepared they are, the harder it hits them.

The coup against Salvador Allende is a case in point. As president he won the support of the Chilean congress for the nationalization of the copper mines, controlled by US companies. But this consensus could not obviate the heavy blow to the US government. As a result, the administration of Richard Nixon – with none other than Henry Kissinger as secretary of state – accelerated the plans for a coup against Allende. For his part, the Socialist president, trusting in Chile's traditions of parliamentary democracy and the Armed Forces' respect for the rule of law, did not prepare to confront the right's offensive with strategies for an alternative power. As a result, when the end came, he found himself surrounded inside the presidential palace, defending alone a legality that the right had long since decided to throw overboard.

The gains that were won by the various reform projects were achieved because they fitted into a long historical period – from the 1930s to the 1970s – when the hegemonic project on both a world and a regional scale was one of progressive, Keynesian regulation and social welfare. The winds were blowing in favour of reform, allowing a certain convergence between the interests of the popular camp and those of a part of the hegemonic bloc.

When the period changed, and regressive projects prevailed – neoliberal ones of deregulation and privatization – the right appropriated the very notion of reform. This came to mean, in the dominant parlance, the dismantling of the state's regulatory role, economic liberalization, open markets and the elimination of employment guarantees.

The very same elite that had dismantled the mechanisms of state regulation, destroyed the public patrimony and left the public purse with impossible debts, now claimed that the key dilemma was the polarization between public and private, or more directly, between state and market.

In this framework, what could a reform project mean? As long as it doesn't challenge the neoliberal model, it will remain just a variant of the same thing. This is what happened with the so-called 'third way' that claimed to be 'the human face of neoliberalism'. It is also the risk that is run by governments that develop important social policies – like the Kirchner, Tabaré Vázquez and Lula administrations and their respective successors, Cristina Fernández in Argentina, Pepe Mujica in Uruguay and Dilma Rousseff in Brazil; they altered the balance of forces in the social field by extending access to basic goods to much wider sectors of the population, but left untouched the hegemony of finance capital, the dictatorship of the private media, and the immense influence of agribusiness, to mention just some of the most important centres of power that dominate our societies. This is the limit of reform today, in the framework of neoliberalism's global hegemony and its consequences in each country. Unless these problems are addressed and solved democratically, these governments could lose the capacity to act that they demonstrated at an earlier stage. That in turn could put a brake on the process of income redistribution and favour a possible return of right-wing governments that take on board some of these policies, strip them of their progressive content and co-opt the beneficiaries.

This is why processes like those in Bolivia, Venezuela and Ecuador – at the same time as they try to implement an anti-neoliberal economic model – seek to combine this with a refounding of the state and the public sphere, so as to allow the emergence of a new bloc of forces in power and a resolution of the crisis of hegemony in a post-neoliberal direction. It is still a process of reforms, but one that leads towards a substantial transformation of the relations of power that underpin the neoliberal state. Without this, it would be difficult to attack the hegemony of finance capital and impose controls on capital movements and foreign exchange, or subordinate the Central Banks to policies of economic and social development.

Returning to the question of reform and revolution, there is no necessary or fundamental contradiction between the two. It depends on the kind of reform, the way and extent to which it affects the key relations of power, as well as on the ability to develop an alternative bloc of forces in which the state – its economic, social and political nature – plays an essential role. Superficial reforms which do not affect the overall balance of power between the main social forces, between opposing political camps, obstruct the processes of profound change in society; they occupy this space and waste social and political energies on mere readjustments – which at present still means readjustments of the hegemonic neoliberal model – instead of helping to build support for the replacement of this model and of the bloc of forces that promotes it.

The defeat of neoliberalism, and the triumph of post-neoliberal projects, depends on this combination between deep reforms and the revolutionary transformation of the old structures inherited by progressive governments in the region. This is where the new mole has unexpectedly and forcefully re-surfaced at the beginning of this new century.

THE THREE STRATEGIES OF THE LATIN AMERICAN LEFT

1. The strategy of democratic reforms

The first strategy developed by the left was based around major structural reforms that would unblock the path to economic development, embodied in the project for import-substitution industrialization. An alliance that subordinated the working class and the left to large-scale, national business, set as its aim the promotion of economic modernization, agrarian reform and national independence. It was a strategy implemented by nationalist forces – Getúlio Vargas in Brazil, Lázaro Cárdenas in Mexico, Juan Perón in Argentina, among others – as well as by forces of the left or centre-left – as in the cases of the Popular Front, led by Pedro Aguirre Cerda (1938), and Popular Unity, led by Salvador Allende (1970), both in Chile.

The fullest expression of this strategy coincided with a long cycle of growth in international capitalism and, in Latin America, with processes of industrial development, under the overarching dominance of export-oriented agricultural and mining interests. Alongside the urban middle classes, the working class grew, helping to expand the domestic consumer market and extend social rights – a process that continued for almost five decades, beginning in the 1930s.

This first main strategy of the left saw its political objec-tive as a transition to national, democratic, industrial societies, in an alliance between the industrial bourgeoisie, the working class and urban middle layers, as a stage prior to the build-ing of socialism. There were two main variants of this kind of project: one led by nationalist forces – examples of which include the Chilean Popular Front, the Mexican PRI, the Bolivian MNR, Peronism, and the Vargas governments in

Brazil; the other led directly by a left coalition – whose main example was the government of Salvador Allende.

Its programmes were centred on economic and social demands, for development and income distribution. It saw the main enemies as big landholdings and imperialism. The premise of the strategy was the existence of a national bourgeoisie with distinct interests from those other two, which would lead a bloc that the left and the workers' movement should join in order to remove the obstacles to national development and democracy.

It was these governments that repeatedly occupied the political space of the left, whether or not they were supported by socialists and communists. The alliance between the latter two forces participated actively in the political struggle until, with Popular Unity's victory in Chile, for the first time the class forces of the left exercised hegemony themselves. Here the strategy took on its most radical form – for this was the only time in the international history of the left that an attempt was made to implement a peaceful transition to socialism.

It was a strategy of institutional transition, without violent breaks, which aimed to incorporate the existing democratic structures, strengthening them and widening them. It sought to democratize economic and social relations, increasing the regulatory role of the state by nationalizing basic industries and controlling the remission of profits abroad.

Popular Unity's programme represented a break with the earlier, stageist strategy (according to which socialism would be preceded by a stage of reforms that would modernize capitalism); it proposed expropriating big capital by nationalizing the 150 largest companies, both foreign and Chilean, thereby giving the state control over the central nervous system of the economy. These nationalized companies would be socialized by setting up councils in which the workers would decide the course of the economy and of each enterprise. Politically, the most important proposal was to unify the Lower House and the Senate in a single chamber.

These proposals were incompatible with existing state structures: the plan was to change these qualitatively, from within. The Allende government had occupied the heart of the state apparatus, that is, its executive branch – albeit with only minority electoral support, of 36.3 per cent in 1970 and 41 per cent in 1973 – but it found itself asphyxiated by these structures. It did not call for a refounding of the state, because it trusted in its democratic character; nor did it call for the building of new power structures, what was called 'popular power', outside the state. The military coup, when it came, marked the demise of this strategy in the most dramatic and complete way possible.

The nationalist governments were either toppled – as happened with Perón and Vargas – or co-opted and reabsorbed, losing their initial momentum – as in the cases of the Mexican and Bolivian revolutions. Getúlio Vargas's suicide in 1954, and the coup against Perón in 1955, coincided with the end of a long parenthesis in world history that began with the 1929 crisis and stretched through the end of the Second World War to the war in Korea. They marked, simultaneously, a change in the nature of the nationalist project of import-substitution – a result of the return of foreign investments on a massive scale (symbolized most clearly by the arrival of the car industry in the region), and at the same time a new phase of the subordination of Latin American capital to processes of internationalization.

This first strategy went into decline, therefore, in parallel with the model of industrialization, when the internationalization of Latin American economies pushed the business class of each country into solid alliances with international capital – a process that would later lead into neoliberalism. Before that, this change made possible the military dictatorships in the Southern Cone, and showed just how ready the dominant bloc was to liquidate the popular movement in order to adhere to economic policies based on exports, the domestic consumption of the rich, and the super-exploitation of labour.

The cycle of Southern Cone military coups – heralded by

the overthrow of Perón and Getúlio Vargas's suicide a year earlier, and later carried through by coups in Brazil, in 1964, in Bolivia, in 1971, in Chile and Uruguay in 1973, and again in Argentina in 1976 – formalized the end of that period, ideologically and politically, and the adherence of the region's national bourgeoisies to a dictatorial, repressive, pro-US posture, that went hand in hand with the internationalization of capitalism in the continent.

The two coups that consolidated this spread of dictatorship across the south of the continent, those in Chile and Uruguay, occurred the same year that is generally held to mark the end of the long wave of growth for capitalism – the longest in its history, described by Eric Hobsbawm as 'the Golden Age of capitalism'. Marked by the oil crisis, it turned the page on a period of history, and with it on one of the strategies of the Latin American left.

2. The strategy of guerrilla warfare

Following the triumph of the Cuban Revolution in 1959, insurrection combined with guerrilla warfare as a strategy of the Latin American left to take power. Guerrilla war had been a characteristic of the Chinese and Vietnamese revolutions, and now made the 'possibility of revolution' a reality in Latin America, through the offices of the 26 July Movement[18] and the Cuban rebel army.

Insurrectional movements had played a part in the wars of independence at the start of the nineteenth century. In the last century, first the Mexican Revolution, later the rebellions of Sandino in Nicaragua and Farabundo Martí in El Salvador, in the 1930s, and then the Bolivian Revolution of 1952, revived the insurrectionary tradition in the continent, with various forms of struggle. But it was the Cuban Revolution

---

18. The 26 July Movement was the revolutionary organization planned and led by Fidel Castro that in 1959 overthrew the government of Fulgencio Batista in Cuba. It took its name from the date of Castro's failed attack on the Moncada Barracks in Santiago in 1953. (*Translator's note*)

that posited armed struggle – in the form of guerrilla warfare – as the second main strategy of the Latin American left.

As had happened before with the Russian and Chinese revolutions, the victorious strategy applied in Cuba exerted an important influence and encouraged numerous imitations, with minor modifications, in various countries. In Colombia, the guerrilla movement had already begun to develop in the 1950s with the FARC. In Nicaragua, the struggle of the Sandinistas had existed for some time before the Sandinista National Liberation Front was formally created in 1961. But in countries like Guatemala, Venezuela, Peru, Bolivia, Argentina, Brazil, Uruguay, Mexico, the Dominican Republic and El Salvador, it was the impetus of the Cuban victory that was mainly responsible for spreading this strategy. In a Latin America that was much more homogeneous than Europe at the time of the Russian Revolution – in spite of the obvious national differences – the Cuban influence spread rapidly, from the cities of Argentina and Uruguay to the rural areas of Guatemala or Peru.

The new strategy was based on the sharp contradictions in the Latin American countryside, the result of the dominance of big landholdings, foreign companies and the primary-export model, which blocked agrarian reform and made this the weakest link of capitalist domination in the continent. In Cuba the guerrillas took advantage of this, along with their mobility, the peasantry's experience of previous victories, the existence of a US-supported dictatorship, and the element of surprise, to achieve victory and open a new strategic path for the Latin American left – one that confronted the end of the cycle of import substitution and liberal democracy, and the proliferation of dictatorships.

There were three different cycles of guerrilla struggle during the four decades after 1959. After that, the conditions that had allowed it to appear as the principal form of struggle for the left in the continent no longer existed. The first cycle developed as an immediate effect of the Cuban victory, in Venezuela, Guatemala and Peru. These last two were, like Cuba, mainly agricultural economies, but with a decisive indigenous presence – although these ethnic groups were seen by the guerrilla movements, in a reductionist way, as peasants. Venezuela, on the other hand, was an oil economy, with only a sparse rural population.

This first cycle could not benefit from the element of surprise, which had made an important contribution to the Cuban revolutionary movement, and for that reason couldn't work after that. On the contrary, the United States, once it got over the surprise, stepped up its Cold War mechanisms, labelling any democratic and popular force as subversive and drawing up a policy to encourage land reform as a condition for inter-governmental aid. With this it sought to reduce the acute level of conflict in the countryside, seen as an essential condition for the emergence of guerrilla movements – which could then swim like fish in this sea. The aim was to isolate these movements from their support base. It was a preventive mechanism similar to the agrarian reforms imposed in Japan and South Korea under US occupation, in order to prevent any repetition of the Chinese Revolution, which had fed off peasant discontent.

On the other hand, in some of these countries the governments still enjoyed a degree of political legitimacy, because they had come to power in non-dictatorial electoral processes, unlike the government of Fulgencio Batista in Cuba. Guatemala was the country most similar to the Cuban case. The version of the victorious Cuban strategy that circulated most widely was a reductionist interpretation – that of Régis Debray in *Revolution in the Revolution.*[19] This favoured voluntarism and militarism, underestimating the mass support enjoyed by the 26 July Movement in Cuba. It gave the impression that the 'small motor' – the initial guerrilla nucleus of twelve fighters – was alone able to create the conditions for the emergence of the 'big motor' – that is, the mass movement. The image of the heroic gesture of those twelve guerrillas who survived

19. Régis Debray, *Revolution in the Revolution*, New York 1967.

the landing of the boat, the Granma, and went on to create the conditions for the revolutionary victory, spread widely. It encouraged groups with no mass roots, in countries whose governments enjoyed some institutional legitimacy, to launch guerrilla struggles which made no headway, because of their social and political isolation.

This first cycle suffered its sharpest defeat in Peru – where it had taken various forms, including the Revolutionary Left Movement (MIR) of Guillermo Lobatón and Luis de la Puente Uceda; the National Liberation Army of Héctor Béjar, and an armed self-defence movement organized by Hugo Blanco – and in Venezuela, both with the MIR of Moisés Moleiro and with the Armed Forces of National Liberation (FALN) of Douglas Bravo. The strategy would re-emerge in Guatemala, however, with the movements led by Yon Sosa and Luis Turcios Lima, because there the conditions more closely resembled those that had existed in Cuba.

This cycle represented the extension of guerrilla warfare as a means of struggle and would mark a new period of left struggle. Its novel aspect, which aimed to lend the struggle a continental dimension, came from Che's plan to organize a guerrilla group in Bolivia, not just as a local revolutionary force, but mainly as a co-ordinating axis for the existing guerrilla movements, and those that were beginning to organize, in Argentina, Uruguay and Brazil.

Che's death and the defeat of his project was in fact the first big defeat for the guerrilla movement in the continent. It closed the first cycle of armed struggle. A second, however, was already gestating, this time centred in the cities of the three countries already mentioned. This development altered key factors, basic principles, of the guerrilla struggle as it had been practised and theorized in Cuba. Countries with largely urban populations, like Argentina and Uruguay, or in the process of rapid urbanization, like Brazil, changed the original rural scenario; the struggle moved closer to its support bases, but it became more difficult to grow from small guerrilla nuclei into the regular, formal structures of an army, because of the very conditions of operating in a dense, urban environment, and the capacity of the repressive forces to operate in that milieu.

On the one hand, the urban context has the advantage of closeness to the nerve centres of power. On the other, it makes it much harder to create liberated zones, which in turn affects the guerrilla forces' ability to grow and leaves them more vulnerable in terms of security. This is what led to the setbacks for the urban guerrilla movement in Argentina, with the Montoneros and the People's Revolutionary Army (ERP), in Uruguay with the Tupamaros, and in Brazil, including all the armed organizations, but especially the most important – the National Liberation Alliance (ALN) and the Popular Revolutionary Vanguard (VPR).

In Argentina and Uruguay, because the development of both popular support and military capability had been greater, the scale of the defeats was also greater. Little remained but the traces of the victims and the destruction of the organized left. Given the radical changes in both the national and international balance of forces that occurred in the years immediately following, these experiences today seem even more distant possibilities, lost in the mists of the past.

The defeats inflicted on the popular camp did not spare any area of opposition, from trade unions to political parties, from universities to civil servants, from social movements to the opposition press, publishers and parliament. They brought a deep, regressive shift in the balance of forces between the fundamental classes, which would prepare the ground for the hegemony of the neoliberal model. The defeat of the popular movement and its organizations, savaged by repression, would also establish the military superiority of the dominant forces.

In the meantime, the old mole of guerrilla struggle would head back to where it started, back to its original habitat in both social and geographical terms, to countries with a mainly rural character. It travelled to Central America and began there the continent's third and last cycle of guerrilla struggles. The Sandinista movement managed to reorganize and reunite the forces it had built up in previous years, and to relaunch the struggle, after Somoza himself helped to open up a space for them by having the main leader of the liberal opposition, Joaquín Chamorro, assassinated.

As mentioned before, Nicaragua reproduced several of the factors that had made victory possible in Cuba. These, together with the breadth of the Sandinistas' international alliances, ended working in favour of a new guerrilla victory in Latin America, twenty years after the triumph of the Cuban Revolution.

Applying similar strategies, the guerrillas in Guatemala and El Salvador relaunched their struggles. Like the Nicaraguans, they managed to unite all the military organizations in each country. However, as had also happened immediately after the Cuban victory, the element of surprise was no longer with them. It should be recalled that the Sandinista victory happened in the same year as the US suffered setbacks in Iran and Grenada.

The effects on the US domestic scene were not long in coming: the Democrats were defeated, the Republicans returned to power with Ronald Reagan and the 'second Cold War' began. Nicaragua was a privileged target of the US counter-attack, so much so that Reagan declared it to be the 'southern flank of the United States'. Nicaragua's frontiers were militarized, especially the northern one with Honduras, which itself became a military rearguard for the United States, just as Laos and Cambodia had done in Indochina.

The United States was intent on preventing the domino effect that had happened in Southeast Asia. To this end, it put all its military might at the service of the Guatemalan and Salvadoran governments, clearly signalling to the guerrilla movements and the international community that Washington would not permit another victory of a hostile movement in the region.

A series of strategic offensives by the guerrilla fronts in both countries were repulsed by government forces, closely supported by the US. This continued until an external factor of unexpected and decisive magnitude fell upon the third cycle of

Latin America's guerrilla struggles: as a consequence of the fall of the Berlin Wall and the collapse of the Soviet Union and the socialist camp, the world returned to a unipolar system, under the hegemony of the very superpower that was confronting the Nicaraguan government and the guerrilla movements in Guatemala and El Salvador. The fall of the Sandinista government – following the invasion of Grenada and, a few years before, the capitulation of the government in Surinam – only accentuated the radical shift in the international correlation of forces.

The Sandinista government had called presidential elections, which were held under conditions of barely concealed bribery by the United States. Holding a sword over the heads of the Nicaraguan people, Washington sent a clear message: vote for opposition candidate Violeta Chamorro, who was linked to the US, and the war will end; vote to keep the Sandinistas in government, and the war will continue. It was at this same time that the Guatemalan and Salvadoran guerrillas realized they could not achieve a military victory, and began to return to institutional, political channels, leaving the armed struggle behind.

Thus concluded the third cycle of guerrilla struggle, and with this a period of the Latin American left in which armed struggle remained the main form of struggle for approximately three decades. At the same time, the defeat of guerrilla movements in countries under military dictatorship, like Argentina, Brazil, Uruguay, Bolivia and Chile (which had brief experiences of guerrilla groups with the MIR and the Manuel Rodríguez Patriotic Front), opened the way for liberal-democratic forces to seize the initiative, take the lead of the opposition and displace the armed groups within the left.

Guerrilla groups continued to exist in countries like Colombia and Mexico, but in a very different national and international context. The FARC, the oldest guerrilla movement in the continent, and the National Liberation Army (ELN) – following the disappearance of the urban guerrilla group, M-19 – continued their trajectory in Colombia, but with much more difficulty than before, as did the local guerrilla groups in Mexico. The Zapatista Army, for its part, is a special case, which emerged as an armed rebellion but does not consider itself a guerrilla movement, nor does it seek victory through armed struggle. As the Colombian case brutally demonstrates, the balance of military forces turned utterly against the guerrilla movements, and in favour of the armed forces of the various countries, now directly supported by Washington. This was one decisive reason why the current social and political movements in the region, including the most representative and radical ones, like the Landless Rural Workers' Movement (MST) in Brazil, the Zapatista National Liberation Army in Mexico, the indigenous movements in Bolivia and Ecuador, have not sought to militarize their conflicts. To do so, as they know, means they would inevitably be decimated by the crushing military superiority of the regular forces, both inside their countries and beyond.

3. The third strategy of the Latin American left

Neoliberal hegemony reshaped the overall framework of political and ideological struggle in Latin America. The radical change in the balance of forces imposed over previous decades – which for some countries meant military dictatorships – was consolidated by the new hegemonic model. The resistance struggles against neoliberalism constituted a new strategy for developing an alternative model. This sought to go beyond the two previous strategies, incorporating and dialectically negating both of them, while shaping itself in the new conditions of neoliberal hegemony.

One of the first features of this new strategy was determined by the nature of neoliberal hegemony itself – in particular, by the creation of a consensus among the elites in favour of profound, liberalizing (counter-)reforms. This consensus was strongly supported and nurtured by the private media which counted on the support of the traditional parties. The social movements were put on the defensive, and resisted, drawing on potentially very widespread popular support, but hampered by this political and media offensive, as well as by the difficulties of their own objective situation (unemployment, precarious jobs, social fragmentation).

A second feature was determined by the adherence of left parties, both social democratic and nationalist, to the neoliberal agenda, leaving the social movements practically alone in their resistance to government policies. The Zapatistas, the MST, the Bolivian and Ecuadorean indigenous movements, all played a prominent part in these struggles of resistance. They were struggles to defend rights under threat, but they adopted militant methods, ranging from the land occupations and marches of the Landless Movement, through the rebellion in Chiapas, to the popular uprisings of indigenous peoples in Bolivia and Ecuador.

As neoliberalism rolled back the state, privatized public enterprises and eliminated rights stretching from formal employment to public education and healthcare, the social movements did what they could to resist. Opposition to the North American Free Trade Agreement (NAFTA) was central for the launch of the Zapatista movement in 1994. The struggle against privatizations was essential to the mobilizations of the Landless in Brazil. Resistance to the privatization of water in Bolivia was the starting point for a whole new stage of the left in that country. Something similar happened in Ecuador, with the power of veto exercised by the social movements over the neoliberal governments and over the signing of a free trade treaty with the United States.

As the neoliberal model began to show its limitations and run out of steam, the carefully manufactured consensus began to break down. Splits emerged between traditional parties, various presidents had to depart without completing their terms in office, or even when they had barely begun them, due to mobilizations launched by the social movements. This was particularly the case in Ecuador, Bolivia and Argentina. In this context, the question of alternatives came to be posed quite concretely for the forces resisting neoliberalism – of how to move from the defensive to the offensive, from struggles of resistance to the dispute for a new hegemony.

There was a shift from the phase of resistance to one where the capacity to veto a government's actions was demonstrated, rendering that government inoperative, but this still did not go as far as developing alternatives. The best example was in Ecuador, whose social movements were able to overthrow three presidents in a row and then block the signing of the Free Trade Treaty with the United States. Lucio Gutiérrez, the third of these presidents, had been elected with the support of these social movements, which took part in his government through the Confederation of Indigenous Nationalities of Ecuador (CONAIE) and Pachakutik, a political movement set up by CONAIE and other social movements.

Such mobilizations combined forms of struggle ranging from territorial uprisings to hunger strikes, road blockades, mass rallies and armed resistance to repression, among others. From this point on, differences began to surface among the anti-neoliberal forces. Some wanted to remain as social movements, justifying themselves with theoretical arguments about the 'autonomy of social movements'. Others sought new forms of articulation with the political sphere, with the aim of being in a position to dispute the unfolding crisis of hegemony. The Bolivian, Ecuadorean and Paraguayan cases clearly fit into this second category; the Mexican and Argentinean into the first.

The argument about 'the autonomy of social movements' found its fullest theoretical expression in the work of John Holloway, who sought to explain the strategy of the Zapatistas, summed up in the title of his book, *Change the World Without Taking Power*.[20] This implied changes in the social sphere at a local level, as illustrated by the Zapatistas' actions in Chiapas. It is an approach that also emphasizes the importance of the grass roots and of building new social structures from the bottom up.

20. John Holloway, *Change the World Without Taking Power: The Meaning of Revolution Today*, London 2002.

It is understandable that social movements should be critical of the traditional parties and the traditional way of doing politics, given the many frustrations they have experienced. The mistake is to give up on politics altogether, believing that an alternative, even one built from the bottom up, could simply avoid disputing the political sphere.

The presence of NGOs (which by definition distance themselves from politics and with which many social movements work closely) strengthens this tendency. The emergence of the World Social Forum, whose 'Charter of Principles' crystallized the separation between social struggle and political sphere, froze the strategy of the popular movements in the phase of resistance, from which it could not escape unless it managed to reconnect these two areas. As long as the social movements limited themselves to the social sphere, they remained on the defensive, unable to create the instruments needed to fight for political hegemony. The 'other possible world' could not be created merely out of grass-roots resistance, but only with new structures of power.

The argument in favour of the 'autonomy of social movements' suffers from two main ambiguities. Firstly, there is a blurring of the differences with neoliberal discourse, in so far as the social movements also choose the state, politics, parties and government as the targets of their attacks. These are positions that are also defended by neoliberals, leading to confusions over what exactly the NGOs and some of the social movements stand for. Secondly, one of the key characteristics of neoliberalism is its wholesale confiscation of rights. To redress this and restore such rights, along with their respective guarantees, can only be done through government policies. Similarly, the regulation of capital movements and financial markets – another central concern of the WSFs – can only be achieved by deliberate state action.

Eight years after the first WSF, that 'other possible world' is beginning to be built in Latin America. In arenas like the Bolivarian Alternative for the Peoples of Our America (ALBA), one of the initial proposals of the WSF, for 'fair trade', is being put into practice, along with other post-neoliberal initiatives like Operation Miracle, the Latin American School of Medicine (ELAM), literacy campaigns and the Bank of the South. The political battles to develop post-neoliberal governments came after the anti-neoliberal forces had suffered several failures. The Zapatistas had retreated into isolation in the south of Mexico, unable to turn their struggle into a national political alternative; the *piqueteros* in Argentina had lost their initial momentum because they had no political expression for their struggles; while Ecuador's indigenous movements had delegated their political representation to a candidate outside their ranks,[21] who then betrayed them even before he took office. Yet while all this was going on, other social and political forces were beginning to outline a new strategy for the left.

This new strategy has had its main developments in Bolivia, Venezuela and Ecuador. The combination of popular uprisings and mass demonstrations gave rise to political-electoral alternatives, distinct from the earlier strategies of insurrectional struggle. However, these new alternatives are also different from the traditional reformist projects, because they propose to implement a programme of economic, social, political and cultural changes, not through the existing power structures but through a refounding of these states. To this end they have united elements from both the reformist strategy and the insurrectionary one, seeking to combine different forms of struggle and to reconnect the social struggle with the political one.

Bolivia is the clearest example of this new strategy. There, the social movements first paralysed the neoliberal governments, then founded their own party, the Movement to Socialism (MAS), in order to establish indigenous hegemony in the political sphere by getting Evo Morales elected as president. The strategy of the Bolivian new left was based on a critique of the traditional left's economism, which had defined the indigenous people as peasants – because they worked the land – and characterized them as small landowners. According

---

21. Lucio Gutiérrez, a former army officer, was elected president in 2002 in alliance with the mainly indigenous party, Pachakutik.

to this scheme, they became subordinate allies of the working class, which was concentrated in the tin mines.

This economism robbed the Aymara, Quechua and Guaraní of their profound and ancient identity as indigenous peoples. It was this critique, elaborated by Álvaro García Linera, the current vice-president of Bolivia, that made it possible to develop a new political subject capable of reconnecting the political sphere with the strength of the mass movement built up since the year 2000, and thereby of fighting for hegemony in the country as a whole.

The path that led nationalist officers to power in Venezuela, and that which got Rafael Correa elected and led to the approval of a new Constitution in Ecuador, both followed this new strategy of the Latin American left.

These processes, which are regenerating the Latin American left, did not happen in countries where the left was traditionally strongest and where, as a result, the repression had been most severe – countries like Chile, Uruguay, Argentina and Brazil. Nor were they led by traditional parties or movements of the left, like communists, socialists or old-style nationalists. And they are not happening in Brazil, where, until recently, there seemed to be some of the most important political and social organizations of the left, like the PT, the CUT, the MST or the WSF, as well as the experiences of participatory budgets.

Venezuela, after the guerrilla movements of the 1960s, saw the creation of a new party, the Movement to Socialism (MAS), which came out of a split in the Communist Party following denunciations of the Soviet invasion of Czechoslovakia. At first its positions were close to those of the Italian Communist Party (PCI), with its theses on Eurocommunism. However, it later followed the collapse of European social democracy into neoliberalism. As such, it took part in the government of Rafael Caldera in the 1990s, with its main leader, Teodoro Petkoff, serving as Economy Minister. Another movement, the Causa R, also emerged, but subsequently lost popular support and failed to regenerate the Venezuelan left.

It was, however, a movement of nationalist – Bolivarian – soldiers that expressed the popular discontent at Carlos Andrés Pérez's 1989 package of neoliberal measures. Coming just after he had been elected on a platform for development, it was met by a massive mobilization against his government, called the *caracazo*, whose repression resulted in several hundred deaths. Something similar happened in Argentina the same year, when Carlos Menem promised a 'strong dose of production' only to assume immediately a neoliberal programme – this time without much popular reaction. Also that year, Fernando Collor de Mello won the presidential elections in Brazil on a neoliberal programme, making 1989 a key year in the implantation of the neoliberal programme in the region. It was of course the same year that the Berlin Wall fell, and the transition to a new period began across the world. Before the year was out, Cuba entered its 'special period', and the following year the Sandinista government fell in Nicaragua.

The military uprising led by Hugo Chávez in 1992, along with the cry of the Zapatistas in 1994, came as the first expressions of resistance to neoliberalism – symptoms of the new kind of force to lead this resistance, in a new and sharper way, encompassing indigenous movements and nationalist military officers. As Chávez himself tells it, the soldiers who rebelled called on the rest of the left to support their movement, but remained isolated and were defeated. Nonetheless his movement had an impact on the political scene, similar to that of the attack on the Moncada barracks in Cuba four decades earlier, or the Sandinistas' first offensive in 1987. They were all military defeats, but political victories.

After the military uprising, the Bolivarian movement was able to recycle itself for political-institutional struggle, with Chávez standing for president of the Republic in 1998. The failure of both the social-democratic governments of Democratic Action (AD), which ended in the impeachment and imprisonment of Carlos Andrés Pérez, and the Christian Democrat government of the other main party, COPEI, with Rafael Caldera as president, signalled the collapse of the two-party system that had characterized Venezuelan politics for three decades.

As a result, in the presidential campaign of 1998, the two favourites were both 'outsiders': Irene Sáez, an ex-Miss Universe who had been mayor of Chacao, a rich neighbourhood of Caracas, and was backed and financed by Venezuelan bankers who had taken refuge in Miami after the banking crisis and subsequent nationalization carried out by Caldera; and Hugo Chávez, who overtook her in the final stage of the campaign and won the election. Chávez immediately called a Constituent Assembly with the idea of refounding the Venezuelan state, thus inaugurating this new strategy of the left.

The anti-neoliberal content, of protest against the neoliberal package and government of Carlos Andrés Pérez, was thus present in the origins of the Bolivarian movement. The anti-imperialist content would come with the oil policy of the new government, when it worked to put fresh life into the Organization of Petroleum Exporting Countries (OPEC) and intensified trade with Cuba, thereby clashing with both the local private media and the Bush administration. This polarization with Washington only accelerated the process.

In 2000, the second year of the Chávez government, as if to celebrate the new century, indigenous revolts broke out in Bolivia and Ecuador. The Bolivian indigenous movement led the Water War, which prevented the privatization of the water distribution system in the city of Cochabamba and its sale to a North American company (the Bechtel Corporation). This began an impressive cycle of struggles that would topple two presidents – Sánchez de Lozada and his vice-president – and lead, five years later, to the election of Evo Morales, the first indigenous person to be elected president of Bolivia.

The rebellions of the Ecuadorean social movements – at first indigenous but later led by urban movements – led to the overthrow of three successive elected presidents who had maintained the neoliberal model. The third of these, Lucio Gutiérrez, had been supported by the indigenous movements, but went back on his programme. This led to a division in the movement. Some sectors stayed in the government, while others broke with it, but were weakened by the defeat and undermined by the fact they had supported the president.

At the same time, other social movements confronted similar challenges: how to bring the strength developed in resistance to neoliberalism to bear at the political level of the dispute over alternatives. To reject the political sphere wholesale because of criticisms of particular political practices was only to 'throw out the baby with the bathwater' and marginalize oneself from the national political dispute.

This is what happened to the Zapatistas, who isolated themselves from the national political struggle. The piqueteros, for their part, after the biggest crisis of the Argentinean state, with the fall of three presidents in one week, adopted the slogan *'que se vayan todos'*[22] in the presidential elections. However, without the strength to overthrow 'them all', they left the field open for Carlos Menem to win the first round by promising to dollarize the economy – with all the consequences that would have had for Latin American integration. In the second round, Kirchner occupied the space vacated by the social movements and was elected president, avoiding the worst. Continuing to defend the 'autonomy of social movements' and failing to understand the need to build alternative hegemonic projects, the piqueteros isolated themselves and saw their enormous capacity for mobilization evaporate, just a few years after they had so spectacularly burst onto the scene.

For these currents, the 'autonomy of social movements' ended up being not a means of regrouping mass forces in order to organize new kinds of political action, nor a way to build alternative forms of power, but simply a refusal to face up to the question of power, a rejection of the battle for hegemony. It represented a retreat to pre-Marxist positions, because the Marxist critique of this kind of autonomism emphasizes the concept of power as a synthesis of economic, social and

---

22. The slogan 'Out with the lot of them' emerged during the mass mobilizations that swept Argentina from December 2001 through much of the following year. (*Translator's note*)

ideological relations, putting power back in command, as the fundamental strategic objective. To abandon the political sphere is to abandon the struggle for power. It serves to protect the supposed 'purity' of the social sphere, directly representing the 'grass roots' against the leadership, which is itself automatically regarded as an illegitimate form of political representation. It means falling back into corporative and fragmented perspectives, an inevitable outcome when the social is split from the political.

The most developed versions of this approach come in the works of Toni Negri, on the one hand, and John Holloway on the other. Both explicitly abandon the struggle for power and hegemony, which are seen as corrupting everything with their forms of representing the popular will. For Negri, the state is a conservative body in relation to globalization. Both theorize existing situations, dealt with in purely descriptive terms; they fail to develop anti-neoliberal strategies and become trapped in the inertia that results from insisting on the autonomy of the social sphere.

Both end up prisoners of a theoretical framework produced by neoliberalism itself – the opposition between public and private, state and civil society, which is a central tenet of neo-liberalism. However, this polarization conceals the core axis of neoliberalism, the principle that drives our age. For behind the category of the private, or of civil society, are hidden very different, indeed counterposed phenomena. Within civil society there coexist trade unions, banks, social movements, drug traffickers and many others. It is not the private sphere that characterizes the neoliberal project. This does not set out to strip power and resources from the state in order to transfer them to individuals, in their privacy, but to throw them into the market. When a company is privatized, it is not the workers who acquire it, but the market which takes control, transferring it to whichever of the competing conglomerates has most financial power.

So what really drives the neoliberal scheme is 'mercantilization' or 'commodification', the turning of everything into commodities, with a price in the marketplace, where everything is bought and everything is sold. Neoliberalism is the most advanced expression of capitalism's historical project, that 'immense accumulation of commodities' with which Marx opens *Capital*.[23] It is a project that began with the end of servitude, making the labour force free – 'naked' in Marx's words – because separated from its realization, which requires the means of production, and turning the land into a commodity too. In this its most recent phase, following the interregnum of the welfare state, things that had been thought of as rights (education, health, etc.) become commodities and are traded in the marketplace. Even goods like water become commodities. Thus the hegemonic sphere in neoliberalism is the sphere of the market.

On the other hand, the opposite pole is not really the state – because this could be a socialist state, a welfare state, a fascist, liberal or neoliberal one. There is, precisely, a dispute over what kind of state. For neoliberalism, it should be a market-oriented, 'financialized' state, which gathers resources from the sphere of production and transfers a large part of them to finance capital through debt payments. But it could also be a state that has been refounded by governments that seek to break out of neoliberalism, developing new structures of power. The state is, therefore, a space in dispute.

The opposite pole to the market sphere is in fact the public sphere, that which revolves around rights and their universalization, and which demands a profound and extensive process of de-commodifying social relations. Democratizing means de-commodifying. It means removing from the marketplace and transferring to the public sphere, rights that are essential to citizenship. It means replacing the consumer with the citizen. In other words, overcoming neoliberalism requires a refounding of the state around the public sphere, incorporating aspects

---

23. This phrase in the first sentence of *Capital, Volume 1*, is itself a quote from Marx's own earlier work, Karl Marx, 'Zur Kritik der Politischen Oekonomie', Berlin 1859, p. 3.

such as participatory budgets, which mean handing fundamental decisions over to organized citizens.

In the neoliberal era, therefore, the theoretical framework is shaped around this opposition between the public sphere and the market sphere, with the state as an area in dispute between the two. On the outcome of this dispute depends the nature of the state and the kind of society that exists.

All the more reason, therefore, for the presence of the state in the fight against neoliberalism, in order to guarantee rights, regulate capital movements and create the spaces for direct participation by citizens in politics and the structures of power. Post-neoliberalism requires a state that has been refounded around the public sphere, and not a polarization against the state in the name of some supposed civil society or private sphere.

To such positions can be added those of the ultra-left. These include intellectual positions that confine their analyses to the level of criticism and denunciations of betrayal, without ever proposing alternatives, and those of doctrinaire groups who merely repeat maximalist demands – abstract calls for the building of socialism – with no grasp of concrete reality, but intent on preserving theoretical principles from the realities that always contaminate them. They do not realize that no revolutionary process ever started from theoretical principles, but rather arrived at these on the basis of demands deeply rooted in the immediate reality – like the Russian Revolution's demands for 'peace, bread and land'. Dogmatic positions like those of the ultra-left have never triumphed anywhere.

In Ecuador, the indigenous movements were slow to recover from their setbacks. In the meantime, from the beginning of 2006, Rafael Correa channelled the strength developed in the anti-neoliberal struggle and occupied the political space they had left free. By the time the indigenous movements launched their main leader, Luis Macas, as candidate, the political landscape had already been defined. Correa won a resounding victory in the second round of the presidential election in November 2006, which allowed him to command the process of building a post-neoliberal order in Ecuador; he called the Constituent Assembly and got the new constitution approved in a referendum in September 2008, along with a series of other measures in line with his assertion that 'the long night of neoliberalism was ending in Ecuador', which was experiencing 'not a period of change, but a change of period'.

At about the same time, in 2006 in Paraguay, Fernando Lugo emerged as the main anti-Colorado leader, at the head of a popular movement to stop the re-election of the then president, Nicanor Duarte. The social movements were slow to take the elections scheduled for April 2008 seriously, and to mobilize for them. When they did, they allowed their differences to prevail and ran separately. Thus weakened, they only got two candidates elected to the national parliament, when their joint vote should have enabled them to elect five times that number. As a result, Lugo didn't win a majority in parliament and had to make alliances with other sectors in order to be able to govern, in addition to deepening his dependence on the Liberal Party. If the social movements had understood better the shift from a phase of resistance to one of hegemonic dispute, and combined politically, they would have strengthened their own position and favoured a post-neoliberal project in Paraguay.

The Bolivian, Ecuadorean and Venezuelan experiences have thus converged on a similar strategy. The aim is to overcome neoliberalism and develop processes of regional integration that strengthen the resistance to imperial hegemony, so as to begin to develop post-neoliberal models. This is the third strategy in the history of the Latin American left.

The big advances made in Latin America in the first years of this century have come about precisely because of the democratization obtained through de-commodification. The economic exchanges between Cuba and Venezuela are a model of what the WSF called fair trade – a trade based on solidarity and complementary capacities, rather than market prices as preached by the World Trade Organization. Venezuela supplies Cuba with the oil it needs, at subsidized prices financed over the long term, while Cuba gives Venezuela practitioners of the best community health care in the world, as well as sports technicians and literacy experts; the latter helped to make Venezuela the second country in the Americas, after Cuba itself, to eradicate illiteracy, according to UNESCO.

These principles were later extended, via ALBA, to exchanges with countries that have far greater needs and much less ability to contribute to others – countries like Nicaragua, Bolivia, Honduras and Dominica, as well as Ecuador and Haiti.[24] It is a system of exchange in which each country gives what it has and receives what it needs, according to the capacities and necessities of each participant. It is the only example of this kind of commerce in the world and is quite different from the market-based criteria of the WTO. It was these principles that gave rise to the ELAM (Latin American School of Medicine) with its original centre in Cuba and another one in Venezuela. This institution, which is is training the first generation of poor doctors in the continent, already has several thousand graduates. Once selected from among the social movements and other popular organizations, including some North American ones, these young people are trained and then return to their own countries to practice health care in the community.

Operation Miracle was set up in similar fashion. Through this, more than a million Latin Americans have received free eye surgery to restore their sight, in Cuban, Venezuelan and Bolivian hospitals. Campaigns against illiteracy have also spread; Venezuela has already completed the process and Bolivia, Nicaragua and Paraguay have all set deadlines for eradicating illiteracy.

All these are examples of de-commodification, as a way of making rights universal. They can only come about through a

---

24. ALBA was set up by Venezuela and Cuba in December 2004. Bolivia joined in 2006, Nicaragua in 2007, Honduras and Dominica in 2008. Ecuador, St Vincent & the Grenadines and Antigua formally joined in 2009, after participating in ALBA as observers for some time. Grenada, Haiti, Paraguay, Uruguay and Syria have all attended as observers. The new administration installed in Honduras after the coup of June 2009 was not recognized by most Latin American governments and immediately cut its ties with ALBA.

break with the central axiom of the neoliberal model, that is, with the primacy of market criteria. They are therefore a step towards the development of a post-neoliberal model.

The development of such a post-neoliberal model, however, demands a prolonged battle for hegemony between the new social-political bloc and the old structures of power. Álvaro García Linera sees this progressing through five different stages.

> a) The crisis of the state is revealed when there emerges 'a politically dissident social bloc whose ability to mobilize and expand territorially has become permanent'.
>
> b) Next, if this dissident bloc manages to consolidate itself as a national, political project that cannot be co-opted by the dominant system, there begins what García Linera calls a *catastrophic stand-off* – which means that this oppositional force shows itself able to develop 'a proposal for power (including programme, leadership and organization, all aimed at assuming state power), and also able to split society's collective imagination between two, different and opposing, political-state structures'.
>
> c) Then comes the formation of a new, governmental, political bloc 'dedicated to using government office to convert opposition demands into acts of state'.
>
> d) There follows the use of the state to build an 'economic-political-cultural power bloc ... combining the ideas of mobilized society with material resources provided by or via the state'.
>
> e) Finally, there is the 'turning point or historical-political fact after which the crisis of the state' is resolved 'through a series of confrontations which either consolidate the new or reconstitute the old' – and this involves not only the political system but also the dominant bloc in power and the symbolic order of state power.[25]

García Linera gives as an example the state crisis in Bolivia that emerged in 2000 with the Water War and which simultaneously reversed the state policy of privatizing public resources and permitted 'the creation of the territorial nuclei of a new, national-popular bloc'. The catastrophic stand-off developed in 2003, when the social movements took the lead in

---

25. Álvaro García Linera, *La potencia plebeya*, Buenos Aires 2008, p. 394.

developing a programme of structural changes and thereby embodied 'a mobilized will to assume state power'. When Evo Morales became president, the old governmental elites were displaced, beginning the development of a 'new economic power bloc and a new redistribution of resources' which continues to the present. The turning point therefore came with the approval of a new constitutional text by the Constituent Assembly, and really took form when this was approved by referendum in August 2008 – although it remains impossible 'to establish with precision the precise moment when this will reach completion'.[26]

This rich classification of the different stages of the battle for hegemony makes it possible to see how the process unfolds and the balance of forces shifts, how the capacity to take the initiative and develop one's own strength changes, and by what means power shifts between the two main blocs in contention.

In the course of this 'state transition', there was a 'modification of the social classes and their ethnic-cultural identities; these classes assumed, first, control of the government and then, gradually, the modification of political power, control over the economic surplus and over the structure of the state'. This new, emerging, power bloc is based economically on urban and agrarian petty-commodity production, especially that of indigenous peasants and small urban producers, as well as a new urban and indigenous intelligentsia, well-known cultural figures, precariously employed workers and a section of the traditional business class, part of it linked to the domestic market. In addition this bloc incorporates a new state bureaucracy, originating in the public universities, which also includes members of trade union networks.

This whole process of state transition, as characterized by García Linera, 'appears as a flux of movements, flexible and interdependent, going backwards and forwards',[27] which affect the structures of power and the balance of both political and symbolic forces.

26. Ibid., p. 395.
27. Ibid., p. 409.

In this third strategy of the Latin American left, there is no subordinate alliance with bourgeois sectors – as there was in the reformist one – nor are the dominant classes annihilated – as in the insurrectionary strategy. Rather, there is a prolonged battle for hegemony, or war of position, in the Gramscian sense. The way the Constituent Assembly was called in Bolivia reflected this dispute. The government could have done it through the direct, proportional representation of the indigenous peoples, for this is what the MAS proposed as a fair way of electing the representatives of the majority of the nation. Such a criterion, however, would have given the government a massive political-electoral victory, resulting in a disconnection between the new political structure and the real relation of economic forces; the elites in the opposition states would certainly have boycotted the new Assembly. This would have created a very difficult situation for the government. Neoliberal policies had greatly weakened the Bolivian state, and a boycott by the wealthiest sectors would have dealt a grave blow to the new administration.

In Venezuela, by contrast, after the government regained control of the state oil company, PDVSA, the state became very strong and big private business, relatively weak. When the latter boycotted the parliamentary elections in 2004, they undermined themselves and reinforced the government. In Bolivia, the state was much weaker. The call for the Constituent Assembly came when the process of renationalizing the country's gas resources was just beginning, and state structures were still badly damaged by neoliberal policies.

The government revised its initial method, mainly because it did not have the means to implement a new Constitution without the participation of any of the forces representing big private capital. The election of the Assembly confirmed a majority for the MAS, but without the two-thirds majority needed to approve the most hotly contested articles. The opposition took part but tried to obstruct the work of the Constituent Assembly, in an effort to recover from their defeat in the presidential election.

The dispute continued in the national and state referenda on autonomy. Here the opposition sought to interpret decentralization in an institutional sense, concentrating solely on the state governments. In a country where state governors had been nominated up until the elections in December 2005, the liberals wanted to confine the democratic debate to the decentralization of regional state administrations; for its part, the government, reflecting the historic demand of the indigenous peoples, proposed a form of decentralization centred on these peoples. With its almost complete monopoly of the private media, the opposition succeeded in imposing its terms and managed, in the states it led, to win support for the referendums. What they really wanted, with their demands for autonomy, was to prevent the agrarian reform already begun by the government from affecting the material basis of their power, namely their monopoly over the land. They also wanted to get their hands on a significant part of the income obtained from the tax on gas. This had gone up from 18 per cent under previous governments to 82 per cent under President Morales, making it a vital resource for the recomposition of the Bolivian state and the implementation of the government's important social policies.

The government again reworked its original proposal, to incorporate aspects of autonomy for regional states. In the end the national referendum strengthened the government. However, the opposition knows that the new Constitution – even after all its compromises – includes basic rights that limit its own power and open the way to multi-ethnic initiatives and institutions that were until recently non-existent.

Other governments were also elected on the strength of opposition to neoliberalism, like those of Lula, Néstor Kirchner, Tabaré Vázquez, Daniel Ortega and Fernando Lugo. None of these, however, took clear steps to break with the model they had inherited, although they did make adjustments and produce significant differences. This was especially true in the first three cases, particularly Brazil, and less so in Paraguay, where Fernando Lugo had great difficulty introducing the changes he wanted because of his lack of a majority in parliament. This aspect makes these countries different from the group mentioned earlier – which includes Venezuela, Ecuador and Bolivia – where the governments *have* broken with the neoliberal model – apart from Cuba, which of course never experienced neoliberalism.

On the other hand, these governments do prioritize regional integration – although Nicaragua is a special case – above the free trade treaties proposed by the United States. Thus they take part in Mercosur, the Union of South American Nations (UNASUR), the South American Defence Council, the Bank of the South, the G20, the continental gas pipeline, and other similar initiatives. In this way, alongside the other governments mentioned above, they contribute not only to strengthening the international space occupied by the South, but also to the development of a multi-polar world. These governments are allies for those that have gone further in breaking with the model and developing more advanced forms of integration, such as ALBA or Petrocaribe.

However, they are also contradictory governments, split between economic policies inherited from past neoliberal governments and foreign policies of regional integration. They are certainly different from their predecessors, while conserving many of the latter's key characteristics, like the primary fiscal surplus and independent Central Banks, etc.

What puts them in the progressive camp is their form of international insertion, which prioritizes integration – unlike the governments of Mexico, Peru, Chile, Costa Rica and others, which have signed free trade agreements with the United States and have thereby mortgaged their future and forfeited any ability to regulate their economies. The latter have joined those vast, free trade-oriented zones where capital moves unimpeded, privatizations abound and the market rules unchecked.

The fundamental dividing line in Latin America, therefore, is not between a good left and a bad left, as some on the right suggest – Jorge Castañeda, for example, whose aim is to divide the left, co-opting the moderate sectors and isolating the more radical ones.[28] This is a position that favours the right.

The fundamental dividing line is between those countries that have signed free trade treaties with the United States, and those that prioritize processes of regional integration. This is the decisive criterion for judging these governments. Among these, of course, as we have said, there are some that advance firmly on the path of a break with neoliberalism and towards the development of a model that we can describe as post-neo-liberal; others simply apply the model more loosely, developing more social programmes and taking part in regional integra-tion projects. Taken together, these countries are creating various kinds of mutual interdependence for the future, while those that signed free trade treaties are completely tied to the United States and its policies.

Any sharpening of the differences between, for example, the governments of Venezuela and Brazil – which diverge in impor-tant respects – would favour the right, isolate the Venezuelan government and possibly push the Brazilian government closer to the United States and its allies in the region. The alliance between moderate governments and more radical ones in the process of integration strengthens both, and the progressive camp as a whole.

At the same time, the new form taken by the battle for hegemony, in an unfavourable international context, means that even in those countries where the governments are advancing in a post-neoliberal direction, the character of the process is not directly anti-capitalist. We call them post-neolib-eral in so far as they are directly counterposed to the processes of commodification dictated by neoliberalism; but they con-tinue to exist alongside big concentrations of private capital – including international and finance capital – while they carry on the battle for a new hegemony, on the domestic market, in parliament, and through a hard-fought struggle to win hearts and minds.

---

28. See Jorge Castañeda, 'Latin America's Left Turn', *Foreign Affairs*, May–June 2006.

The further they are able to take the aspects of de-commodification, of socialization within the nationalized industries, of building popular power, of building a consensus in favour of socialization, of restoring the importance of labour and fighting against alienation, the greater will be their chances of moving beyond post-neoliberalism towards anti-capitalism and socialism.

To declare that only socialism can put an end to neoliberalism is to fail to grasp the extent of the historic retreat implied by the shift from the previous period of history to the present one. It was a retreat not only for socialism as a general objective, but also for the distinct forms of anti-capitalist consciousness, for the centrality of the world of labour and for the different kinds of popular organization. What is needed is not just an act of will, but the rebuilding, in new ways, of the objective and subjective conditions for anti-capitalist struggle. And one of these new ways, the most important in the current period, is the anti-neoliberal struggle and the building of post-neoliberal alternatives.

An affirmation like this fails to take account of the balance of forces that really exists in the region and in the world, which has to be our starting point. The left, and especially the ultra-left, has great difficulty accepting the setbacks suffered. It prefers to reiterate general theoretical theses, principles and dogmas, as if these operated directly in history as they do in books, without the concrete conditions of class confrontation getting in the way. It has difficulty accepting what Lenin and Gramsci understood so clearly, namely, that 'the truth is concrete'. It is therefore incapable of comprehending the dynamics of new, concrete experiences like those in Venezuela, Bolivia and Cuba, and as a result misses the most important thread of what is going on in the region.

No revolutionary process ever developed as a result of attempts to impose general, abstract theses on a complex and always heterodox reality. In Russia, as noted earlier, the goal was to obtain 'peace, bread and land'; in China, to expel the invaders and carry out an agrarian revolution: in Cuba, to oust

Batista; in Vietnam, to expel the invaders and win national independence; in Nicaragua, to overthrow the Somoza dictatorship.

These objectives cleared the way for achieving other, more profound ones – anti-capitalist in some cases, anti-imperialist in others – because the revolutionary leaderships proved able to develop this dynamic out of those initial, concrete objectives. In Russia at the beginning of the twentieth century, that meant going beyond the winning of peace by breaking international alliances with the imperialist powers; turning the demand for bread into the nationalization and socialization of large-scale industries; or developing the need for land into the agrarian revolution. Something similar happened in other revolutionary processes, through the transitional dynamic of concrete demands that were deeply felt by broad layers of the people, and which also served to establish alliances, build the new hegemonic social bloc and isolate the dominant regime.

Any strategic proposal has to be anchored, first and foremost, in concrete reality, in the specific dynamic of the great confrontations of the time. It has to take account of the fact that all processes of transformation involve aspects that are new and heterodox, which need to be understood, rather than reduced to theoretical axioms which never seem to have been verified in any specific situation. Fidel Castro said that all revolutionary processes should be radical, in the Marxian sense: that they should go to the root of things. But they should never be extremist, in the sense of taking one aspect of reality and giving it extreme importance, without understanding the significance of each historical process as a whole.

The term post-neoliberal is descriptive. It refers to new processes, that arise in response to the deep and repressive changes effected by neoliberalism, but have not yet acquired a permanent form. This is what we see in Venezuela, Bolivia and Ecuador. They do not constitute a specific, historical phase, distinct from capitalism and socialism, but rather a rearrangement of the power relations between social classes, one that encourages the emergence of a new social bloc at the head of particular, *sui generis* historical processes, in circumstances that are much more favourable to the popular forces. Their destiny will be decided by the concrete experience of building post-neoliberal states.

5

The Future of Latin America

PHASES OF THE ANTI-NEOLIBERAL STRUGGLE

The struggle against neoliberalism already has a history. It has been through several phases – from resistance to the development of alternatives – and now faces a new situation, that of a counteroffensive from the right, and the respective responses from the left.

It was in 1994, the same year as the North American Free Trade Agreement (NAFTA) came into effect, that the Zapatistas began resistance to the new hegemony. In 1997, Ignacio Ramonet, in an editorial in *Le Monde Diplomatique*, called for struggle against the 'single orthodoxy' and the Washington Consensus. The World Social Forum in 2001 invited people to build 'another possible world'. The demonstrations against the World Trade Organization (WTO), which had begun in Seattle in 1999, showed the extent of the disconnection between the new hegemonic model and the popular potential for struggles against it. This was a phase of resistance to the negative turn, of gigantic historical proportions, which resulted from the move from a bipolar to a unipolar world, and from the regulatory model to the neoliberal one.

At government level, the consolidation of the neoliberal model came with the shift from the initial right-wing leadership (Pinochet, Reagan and Thatcher) to a second generation, called by some the 'third way' (Clinton, Blair, Fernando Henrique Cardoso), thus occupying the entire political spectrum. The dominance of this force first began to be checked with the election of Hugo Chávez as president of Venezuela in 1998, a process which from then on was concentrated in Latin America. When the model's principal protagonists suffered successive electoral defeats (Cardoso, Menem, Fujimori, Carlos Andrés Pérez and the PRI), its failure became evident.

Nonetheless, the popular reaction against neoliberalism reflected in the electoral victories that followed that of Chávez – Lula (2002), Néstor Kirchner (2003) and Tabaré Vázquez (2004) – did not unfold in quite the way expected. Although these governments won election against hard-line, neoliberal predecessors, they did not move to break with the neoliberal model as such. On the contrary, they maintained it, applying it with varying degrees of flexibility, mainly depending on the relative weight they gave to social policies.

Brought together by their shared support for regional integration – first and foremost through Mercosur – and the defeat of the FTAA, to which they actively contributed, these new governments showed significant differences from their predecessors. They helped create an unprecedented situation in the region, with the simultaneous existence of an assortment of different kinds of government, all opposed to the free trade policies preached by the United States, as well as its policy of 'unending war' – which Colombia was the only country in the region to support.

The victories of Evo Morales (2005) and Rafael Correa (2006), along with the creation of ALBA, the Bank of the South, the continental gas pipeline and the entrance of Venezuela and Bolivia into Mercosur, broadened and strengthened an axis of governments that not only supported regional integration but were also beginning to develop post-neoliberal models. Fernando Lugo's election in Paraguay (2008) and Mauricio Funes's in El Salvador (2009) further extended the camp of progressive governments in the continent.

Nonetheless, from 2007, after being rather taken by surprise by the spread of progressive governments across the region, the right recovered its ability to take the initiative. The progressive governments had managed to take electoral advantage of the social discontent at neoliberal policies – thus exploiting the weakest link in the neoliberal chain.

In order to retake the initiative, the right – both the old, oligarchic right and the social-democratic currents that adhered to neoliberalism – resorted to the two areas where its hegemony and its strength remained intact: the economy and the media, both of which it controlled. Its counteroffensive took slightly different forms in different countries, but the elements were the same. Criticism was levelled at the state and its regulatory functions, at tax policies and at regional and South-South integration initiatives. Attention was directed to issues like corruption (always in relation to government and the state), supply shortages, the autonomy of regional governments against state centralization, and supposed 'threats' to 'press freedom' (always identified with the private media).

In Brazil, there were campaigns of denunciation against the Lula government. In Venezuela, after the attempted coup in 2002, the right began to campaign in defence of the private monopolies in the media, and to denounce corruption and food shortages. In Bolivia, the attacks were directed at land reform, the new Constitution and the introduction of new taxes on gas exports to finance social policies carried out by the government. In Argentina, the target was price regulation and supply problems, while in Ecuador it was the new Constitution and new forms of state regulation. In addition to these, the right could count on the two main right-wing governments in the region – Mexico and Colombia.

The right also went back on the offensive in the economic domain, having been on the defensive during the years of international economic growth, when the income from foreign trade could easily be used to finance social policies. Now it began again to warn of the danger of rising inflation and the need for fresh adjustments, with higher interest rates, giving priority to monetary stability at the expense of economic growth. The *Economist* magazine expressed the hope that, with the change in the international situation, the right might return to the fore, drawing on two issues dear to conservative thinking: inflation and law and order. The Latin American examples of this are significant.

This new phase, from 2008, was marked by renewed confrontation between progressive governments and the right-wing opposition, both politically and ideologically. The attempts to discredit the role of the state became the central axis of debate between right and left.

Today in Latin America there are a number of countries that follow the prescriptions of the 'minimum state'. Mexico began a process of privatizing the state oil company, Pemex, putting itself at the forefront of neoliberalism's fresh push for privatization. Peru (which joined the ranks later), Chile and Costa Rica remain the success stories of this current – although they have had to repair gaping holes in their private pension systems, once models for the region.

On the other hand, there are a number of countries that seek to rebuild their states on post-neoliberal or post-liberal foundations. That means they seek new forms of political representation, that go beyond liberal formalisms, as in the cases of Venezuela, Bolivia and Ecuador – the latter two seeking to found pluri-national, multi-ethnic, multicultural states.

Between these two groups, several countries – like Brazil, Argentina, Uruguay and Paraguay – have implemented certain levels of state regulation, without going back to the sort of state that existed before neoliberalism. They have slowed down the earlier processes of privatization, encouraged the growth of formal employment, and regenerated public administration and services.

Evo Morales's victory in the August 2008 referendum, by an

ample margin, showed that mass support was still there. So did the levels of popular backing for Rafael Correa and Lula. The elections of Fernando Lugo in Paraguay, Mauricio Funes in El Salvador and then Dilma Rousseff to succeed Lula in Brazil showed that the consolidation and expansion of progressive governments in Latin America had not come to an end, in spite of the offensives of the right. Dilma Rousseff's victory in Brazil was the result of enormous popular support for the Lula government, in which she had played the role of central coordinator; her success means that by the end of her mandate, the PT will have ruled Brazil for twelve years.

The future of neoliberalism in the continent is not yet decided. The model remains hegemonic. Mexico, Peru, Colombia and Chile continue to practise it in orthodox form, while it survives in various different forms in countries like Brazil, Argentina and Uruguay. In the end its destiny will depend on the capacity of the first two of these to move beyond it. Brazil in particular, because of the strength of its economy, rising prestige and the possibility that its current government will continue and deepen the course set by its predecessor, could play a key role in the regional balance of forces between neoliberal hegemony and the projects that promise an alternative.

The consolidation and expansion of ALBA is another strategic element for the future of the continent, and even for the future of a post-neoliberal order on a world scale. At first this initiative advanced at the points of least resistance, where neoliberalism had never existed – like Cuba – or where it had failed before it could really take hold, like Venezuela, Bolivia and Ecuador, whose neoliberal governments were toppled by popular movements. Other countries joined, attracted by the more favourable terms of trade, which began to demonstrate the superiority of principles like solidarity and complementarity over those of free trade. Petrocaribe further reinforces this argument, and makes it possible to imagine a future favourable to the expansion of ALBA.

One limit to such expansion results from the high degree of internationalization of the region's economies, especially the most developed among them, chiefly Mexico, Brazil and Argentina. In the case of the latter two, this could also limit the extension of Mercosur. While the regional integration projects partly overlap with the interests of big international companies and internationalized, local companies, these might prefer free trade treaties, which allow them to increase their integration with the international market and with the central capitalist powers. However, when these slow down in comparison with intra-regional trade and with the big economies of the South, especially China and India, that encourages these big companies to take a closer interest in some aspects of the integration process, especially those that give them access to bigger markets and promise fresh investments.

Some initiatives, like the Bank of the South, the continental gas pipeline, UNASUR, the South American Defence Council and even Mercosur, are areas of dispute over the future shape of South American integration, which still does not have any clear statement of where it is going or how it should proceed.

FOR A POST-NEOLIBERAL LATIN AMERICA

How far can this new push for change in Latin America develop and deepen its anti-neoliberal models in a world still dominated by free trade, the WTO, the World Bank and by mainly conservative powers, of which Europe is one example and the United States another?

Soviet socialism was the first big driving force for change in the last century, but it failed because it never managed to break out of its initial isolation. When it did, this was not in the direction of developed Europe, of the centre of capitalism, of the countries where the forces of production were most highly developed, but in the opposite direction, towards backward Asia and Latin America, and one of the less developed countries of this continent, Cuba. What is the potential of the anti-neoliberal struggle in Latin America? Is it limited to anti-neoliberal reactions within a capitalist framework, or does it have the potential for much deeper change?

Although recent, the anti-neoliberal struggle already has a history and has gone through several stages. It began with the *caracazo*, the popular resistance against President Carlos Andrés Pérez's neoliberal package in 1989, continued with the Zapatista rebellion in 1994 and developed further with the mobilizations of landless peasants in Brazil, with the indigenous struggles in Ecuador, Bolivia and Peru, and with the struggles of the unemployed or piqueteros and the factory occupations in Argentina.

The election of Hugo Chávez in 1998, combined with the crises in Brazil (1999) and Argentina (2001–2002), functioned as a moment of transition to a second phase. This resulted from a crisis of hegemony and involved a political battle for government and for the implementation of alternative policies. If the social movements played a leading role in the first phase, the shift to the second phase presented the anti-neoliberal forces with a challenge: how to win back the political arena through either traditional or novel ways of combining the social and the political spheres.

The phase that followed was marked by a striking series of electoral victories based on popular rejection of neoliberalism. These involved the election or re-election of governments that, in one way or another, came to form a bloc of progressive forces in Latin America and open up an alternative to the governments that had occupied virtually the entire political landscape of the continent during the previous decade.

These forces advanced along neoliberalism's lines of least resistance – especially in areas of social policy, devastated by neoliberalism, and of regional integration, given the failure of free trade policies in the region. They also made some progress in restoring the capacity of the state – which had been rolled back by neoliberalism – to implement regulations and guarantee and extend social rights.

This was the period that brought the most sweeping progressive changes ever experienced on the Latin American political and ideological scene – only comparable to the cycle of independence wars, two centuries earlier. Neoliberalism was caught unprepared to face challenges in the political arena, while the United States was bogged down in its policy of 'unending war'.

As a result, in the few years between 1998 and 2008, governments of this kind came to office in eight Latin American countries, with important defeats in just four (Mexico, Peru, Colombia and Costa Rica).

After this period of extension of these new kinds of government, there began to be signs of a reaction, of a counteroffensive by the right. The two phases overlap in time. While Fernando Lugo's election was putting an end to more than six decades of Colorado rule in Paraguay, and Mauricio Funes was leading the FMLN to victory in the March 2009 presidential elections in El Salvador, the right-wing offensives continued to gather steam, taking advantage of contradictions besetting many of these governments.

This reaction began with the attacks by the Venezuelan right – and the attempted coup of April 2002 – soon followed by the denunciations of corruption against Lula in 2005. Both cases heralded the new line-up of the right bloc, with ideological and political leadership in the hands of the big, private media, and the parties of the right acting as their agents. The Bolivian right took advantage of the Constituent Assembly to regroup, with its base in the economically dynamic eastern part of the country.

The right regained the initiative against Lula with denunciations of corruption – supported by its tight monopoly of the private media and by the bloc of right-wing parties – which looked like they might lead to impeachment. However, the support obtained through his social policies allowed the president to survive the crisis and use those same social policies to consolidate his position. He won re-election and by the end of his second term enjoyed popularity ratings of 87 per cent, with a rejection rate of just 4 per cent.

Hugo Chávez faced a right-wing opposition that had swung between boycott and electoral participation. When it put its trust in the latter, institutional path, it was able to reunite and strengthen itself, to the point of defeating the government in the referendum on constitutional reform in December 2007. When Cristina Fernández succeeded her husband, Néstor Kirchner, as president of Argentina, she suffered strong opposition attacks for her proposal to raise levies on agricultural exports. The death of Néstor Kirchner rather than lessening the possibilities for Cristina Kirchner's continuation in office, strengthened her candidacy for a second term.

After managing to win approval for his proposal for a new constitution, Evo Morales suffered the most violent opposition attacks, which for a time undermined his support. Yet by 2009 he was again able to win large majorities, in the Constitutional Referendum in January and the presidential re-election in December.

Up until now, the opposition blocs have displayed a clearly restorationist response to the advances secured, in greater or lesser degree, by the progressive governments. Their positions advocate a return to the 'minimum' state, lower taxes, renewed privatizations, reduced public spending, more open markets and more precarious conditions of employment. It is a packet of measures that does not add up to a programme, but merely serves to rally the discontented and those displaced from power.

What will happen to Latin America in the future? How far are the changes irreversible? What kind of regression could the region suffer, if the current political processes are not consolidated?

One possibility is the continuation of the present governments and, as a result, the consolidation of the processes of integration, leading to a single regional currency, coordinated Central Banks and the development of the Latin American Parliament,[1] along with advances in each country's economic model and increased possibilities of a rupture leading to the

---

1. The Latin American Parliament (Parlatino) was formally created in 1964, and actually established in 1987. Most of its members are elected by the legislatures of the different member countries, and it has few powers. However, some countries, like Venezuela, have sought to strengthen the body and elect their representatives directly, alongside the members of their own national assembly.

development of alternative models. Internationally, Latin America would make an important contribution to the development of a multipolar world, based on stronger regional integration.

It has to be remembered that anti-neoliberal strategies – the only ones possible, given the current national and international balance of forces – entail a prolonged battle for hegemony. That means they involve neither a subordinate alliance with leading fractions of the bourgeoisie – as the traditional reformist strategy did – nor the annihilation of the adversary, as the armed struggle strategy did. This encourages the recomposition of anti-neoliberal and anti-capitalist social subjects, and at a more advanced stage, once the state has been refounded, it crystallizes a new balance of forces and of power between the major social blocs.

Some regional integration projects present serious problems and could be abandoned, depending on how far the current governments advance. This is the case with the continental gas pipeline, the Bank of the South and the South American Defence Council, among others. There is popular support on a level never before experienced by the left in the region, above all thanks to the social policies carried out by the progressive governments, which sets them apart from the neoliberal governments.

It is this support which confronts the economic and media power of the right, and means that elections across the region occur in very similar circumstances. The candidates may be more or less radical, but the scenario is always the same. On one side, there is a neoliberal bloc supported by the powerful, private monopoly of the media; on the other, the social policies of the governments. The media monopoly 'manufactures' public opinion – in the sense that Chomsky gives the term in *Manufacturing Consent*[2] – and defines day after day the themes that are most important for the country, passing off its interpretation as if it were the general interest; yet when the electors

---

2. Noam Chomsky and Edward S. Herman, *Manufacturing Consent: The Political Economy of the Mass Media*, New York 2002.

have their say, it is defeated. As one Brazilian journalist put it after he and the paper he worked for had been defeated in the 2006 presidential elections: 'The people have defeated public opinion.'

Given their importance, what happens to the processes in Venezuela, Bolivia and Ecuador is vital to the political and ideological future of the region. Nonetheless, because of their size, in the last analysis this depends on what will happen to the current governments in Brazil and Argentina, and on the fate of Mexico. Either way, it is clear that the future shape of Latin America in the twenty-first century depends on what happens to the progressive governments that currently exist in the region.

Yet what bearing could Latin America have on the situation of neoliberalism and capitalism in the world? How far does the region's reduced economic weight – a result of neoliberal policies – take importance away from everything else that is going on here, in terms of its impact on the overall destiny of the world in the decades to come?

We could say, to summarize the essential aspects, that the world today is dominated by three main axes, three great monopolies of power: the power of arms, the power of money and the power of the word. Latin America may contribute, in some respects, towards overcoming these power structures, even if, by itself, it does not have sufficient weight to alter them substantially. Nonetheless, through alliances with India, China, South Africa, Russia or Iran, and with the intensification of South–South exchange, the continent may acquire a new weight through a new kind of presence on the world stage – a world stage that will itself have changed. To a certain extent this is already the case, as has been shown by the region's relative ability to withstand the latest economic crisis. It has obviously been affected, but in a much milder way than in earlier crises.

The struggle against the power of arms means releasing the world from US hegemony. Latin America's contribution here has been to oppose the empire's policies of 'unending war'.

This was shown very clearly when the United States failed to persuade even its close allies in the region, Chile and Mexico, to back its plans for an invasion of Iraq in the UN Security Council. Colombia, the epicentre of 'unending war' in Latin America, finds itself isolated – as was shown after its aggression against Ecuador, when it won the support only of Washington and was condemned by the other countries, as well as by the OAS (Organization of American States). Latin America is the only region of the world to carry out processes of integration that are relatively autonomous from the US and to develop alternatives to the free trade treaties proposed by Washington and the WTO. It also has some of the few governments in the world which frontally oppose and challenge North American imperial hegemony: Cuba, Venezuela, Bolivia and Ecuador.

However, this is not enough to develop a political and military counterweight to the United States. At most, it is an example of resistance, building an integrated area in a region with little weight in the new world economic order. The creation of UNASUR, a project of integration for the whole of South America, and of a South American Defence Council, both without the participation of the United States, as well as the first sessions of the Mercosur Parliament, point towards broader forms of integration with fresh potential.

The importance of the region as a whole comes from its energy resources (especially oil, but also gas) and its agribusiness (with soya exports leading the way, but with production for the domestic market also growing constantly), alongside these integration processes that boost its political influence in international negotiations. But it is the processes of rupture with the neoliberal model and the alternative forms of trade, like ALBA, that make the region a reference point for debates about alternatives to neoliberalism, such as those developed in the World Social Forum and in its regional and thematic forums. Leaders with different kinds of influence in different milieus, like Hugo Chávez and Lula, along with the Bolivian and Ecuadorean processes, indicate the political dimension of Latin America's growing importance in the world.

All the same, there are weaknesses in Latin America's post-neoliberal processes, and one of these weaknesses is their relative isolation in the world. In the absence of strategic allies, the continent is obliged to link up with countries that have some kind of conflict with the United States, like Russia, Iran, China, and Belarus. What is more, the countries that have taken concrete steps to break with the neoliberal model are not the relatively most developed ones in Latin America, although they can count on Venezuela's oil as an important economic factor in their favour.

Ideologically, Latin America can throw up proposals for debate, like the pluri-national and multi-ethnic state, socialism of the twenty-first century and integration through solidarity, exemplified by ALBA. However, the means to disseminate such ideas in a way that is adequate to the needs of the political moment, simply do not exist, even within each of these countries. They have difficulty competing with the single orthodoxy and its basic propositions, which are repeated over and over again by the monopoly media.

Latin American critical thought, which has a long tradition of impressive interpretations and theoretical and political proposals, now faces new challenges, with old themes reappearing in new forms: the new nationalism and processes of regional integration; indigenous peoples and the new model of accumulation; processes of socialization and de-commodification; the new forms to be assumed by the state and the nature and functions of the public sphere; the political future of the continent.

In some countries, the most significant of which is Bolivia, there is a rich and renewed process of theoretical reflection and elaboration on the processes that are unfolding. In others, the most extreme case being Venezuela, there is an enormous gulf between the academic intelligentsia and the process lived by the country. In others still, like Brazil, Argentina and Mexico, in spite of their strong academic systems and the high quality of their intellectual production, a large part of this work has no connection with the main political and social struggles these countries are experiencing. The theoretical potential that exists in the region could make an important contribution to the development of post-neoliberal alternatives, if only it can find new ways of engaging with these contemporary historical experiences.

At the beginning of this new century, Latin America is living through a crisis of hegemony of enormous proportions. The old is struggling to survive, while the new has difficulty in replacing it. The objective conditions for the end of neoliberalism already exist. Yet countries like Brazil, Argentina and Uruguay have retained the model, applying it more loosely, continuing the financial policies but not the economic ones. In the process, they have managed to return their economies to cycles of growth, something the preceding governments had been unable to do, for all their orthodox application of the model. Mexico, which stills follows the orthodox path, has not managed to advance economically, and even Chile – a model of how to apply the neoliberal approach – has seen the cycle of Concertación governments come to an end.

The difficulties encountered in developing social and political subjects able to break with neoliberalism are largely the result of the real obstacles faced by any attempt to leave neoliberalism behind. When steps were taken to develop new kinds of political and ideological leadership for the anti-neoliberal struggle, real progress was made in this direction. The outcome of the crisis of hegemony will push the future of the continent in the direction that the social, political and ideological struggles decide.

Index

Ação Libertadora Nacional
(ALN). *See* National
Liberation Alliance (Brazil)
Acción Democrática (AD), 21,
128
Aguirre Cerda, Pedro, 9, 112
Alencar, José, 55
Alfonsín, Raúl, 14
Algeria, 95
Aliança Libertadora Nacional
(ALN). *See* National
Liberation Alliance (Brazil)
Alianza Bolivariana para los
Pueblos de Nuestra América
(ALBA), 18, 41, 125–26,
135, 140, 146, 149, 156, 157
Allende, Salvador, 8, 9, 10,
19, 101–3 passim, 109–14
passim
Allessandri, Jorge, 9
Alliance for Progress, 8, 10

ALN. *See* National Liberation
Alliance (Brazil)
Alvarado, Velasco, 8, 72
Amin, Samir, 97
Anderson, Perry, 39, 90–93
passim
Angola, 89
Argentina, 7–24 passim, 123–30
passim, 139, 148; coups,
19, 20, 44, 114–15; crisis
of 2001–2002, 22, 32, 151;
Cuban Revolution and,
116; Great Depression and,
29–30; industrialization
projects, 20; internationalized
economy, 150; nationalism,
9, 12, 21, 73, 82, 108, 112;
neoliberalism, 12, 23–24,
34–35, 37, 49, 73, 149,
158; oil, 13–14; piqueteros,
15, 130; post–World War II

Escuela Latinoamericana de
Medicina (ELAM). *See* Latin
American School of Medicine
Europe, 11–12, 36–39 passim,
68–70 passim, 92, 127, 150;
fascism, 69, 70; World War
II, 95, 98

FALN. *See* Armed Forces
of National Liberation
(Venezuela)
Farabundo Martí National
Liberation Front (FMLN),
152
FARC. *See* Fuerzas Armadas
Revolucionarias de Colombia
(FARC)
Fernández, Cristina, 3, 110, 153
France, xi, xiii, xiv, 9–12
passim, 38, 39, 95
Frank, Andre Gunder, 97
Free Trade Area of the Americas
(FTAA), 3, 28, 40, 57, 146
Frei, Eduardo, 8, 9, 10, 102
French Communist Party. *See*
Parti communiste français
(PCF)
Frente Sandinista de Liberación
Nacional (FSLN). *See*
Sandinista National
Liberation Front
Friedman, Milton, 93n11
Fuerzas Armadas de Liberación
Nacional (FALN). *See* Armed
Forces of National Liberation
(Venezuela)
Fuerzas Armadas
Revolucionarias de Colombia
(FARC), 116, 121–22
Fujimori, Alberto, 3, 15, 18, 20,
39; defeat of, 23, 146

Fukuyama, Francis, 24, 93
Funes, Mauricio, 147, 149, 152

García, Alan, 28, 41
García Linera, Álvaro, 75, 100,
106, 107, 127, 136–37
García Márquez, Gabriel, 11
German Communist Party, 104
Germany, x, 38, 83, 99; Nazism,
88, 104; reconstruction, 94,
95–96; Soviet Union and,
86–87. *See also* Berlin Wall
Gil, Gilberto, 57
Goldman, Pierre, xiv
Gomes, Ciro, 54
González, Felipe, 38
Goulart, João, 17, 44
Gramsci, Antonio, 47, 78, 83,
84
Great Britain, 10, 38, 39, 92,
95, 146
Greece, 95
Grenada, 10, 18, 19, 120, 121
Guatemala, 10, 17, 18, 108,
120, 121; Cuban Revolution
and, 116–17; revolutionary
movements, 118
Guevara, Che, 17, 18, 19, 78,
118; *Guerrilla Warfare*,
71–72
Gutiérrez, Lucio, 24, 40, 124,
129

Haiti, 135
Hegel, G. W. F., x
Hitler, Adolf, 88
Hobsbawm, Eric, 94, 115
Ho Chi Minh, 78, 83
Holloway, John, 76, 124, 131
Honduras, 11, 72, 120, 135
Hungary, 95